THE PREFERRED PROVIDER'S HANDBOOK
Building a Successful Private Therapy Practice
in the Managed Care Marketplace

THE PREFERRED PROVIDER'S HANDBOOK

Building a Successful Private Therapy Practice in the Managed Care Marketplace

William L. Poynter, M.S.W., B.C.D.

BRUNNER/MAZEL PUBLISHERS · NEW YORK

Library of Congress Cataloging-in-Publication Data

Poynter, William.
    The preferred provider's handbook: building a successful
private therapy practice in the managed care marketplace /
William Poynter.
       p.   cm.
    Includes index.
    ISBN 0-87630-708-X
    1. Psychotherapy—Practice—United States.   2. Managed care
plans
    (Medical care)—United States.   3. Psychotherapy—United States—
    Marketing.   I. Title.
    RC465.6.P68   1994
    616.89'14'0688—dc20   93-38869
                                                CIP

This book contains the advice and experience of expert authorities from many fields. But the use of a book is not a substitute for legal, accounting, or other professional services. Consult a competent professional for answers to your specific questions.

Published by
BRUNNER/MAZEL, INC.
19 Union Square West
New York, New York 10003

Manufactured in the United States of America

10 9 8 7 6 5 4 3 2

With deep gratitude,

this book is

Dedicated

to

RICHARD F. JOHNS

for his

Unmanaged Care,
Patience, Fortitude, and Wisdom
(and his computer skills!)

Contents

Prologue

Over the past few years corporate America has turned overwhelmingly toward behavioral managed care as the preferred payment mechanism for providing psychotherapy to their employees and dependents. Early indications all point to a continuation of that trend as the federal government looks to "managed competition" as the framework for national health care. Managed care constitutes a revolution in behavioral health care financing. And it leaves psychotherapists with a desperate need to catch up. This book is the mechanism for catching up.

From a base of only a few companies in the mid-1980s, the growth of managed behavioral health care has been explosive. Alex R. Rodriguez, M.D., senior vice president and chief medical officer for Preferred Healthcare, states "The 'story' is . . . the phenomenal movement of payers towards managed care, such that in excess of 80 million persons are expected to have their EAP, mental health, and substance abuse benefits managed by specialty managed care organizations by the end of 1993. This growth will continue well into the 1990's."[1] Joe Duva of the consulting firm of Ernst and Young estimated in August of 1992 that by that date over 90% of employers had moved into managed care at least to some degree.[2] The Health Forecasting Group of Santa Clarita, Ca. has predicted that there will be at least a 50% drop in indemnity plans by 1995, and managed care will "absolutely rule" the marketplace.[3]

As a result of this massive shift in mental health care financing, psychotherapists in private practice have increasingly sought to sign contracts with managed care companies. But many are confused about how to get contracts and how to understand them. And, frequently, therapists have even been locked out of contracts by full provider panels who have no room for more providers.

In March of 1992, *Psychotherapy Finances* newsletter reported in their annual practice survey that 66% of the therapists interviewed had signed contracts for some form of preferred reduced-fee care.[4] By June, 1992, *Open Minds Newsletter* reported that the average provider in their survey of almost 2,000 behavioral health therapists had almost five contracts with managed behavioral health care programs, offering an average discount of 24% from their regular fee.[5] Therapists who have contracted with managed care companies have found that those contracts are beginning to constitute major portions of their caseloads—an average of 25% of patient hours in 1991, according to a survey conducted by *Managed Care Strategies* and reported in September, 1992.[6] As therapists have begun to derive major portions of their incomes from M.C.O. (Managed Care Organization) contracts, they have begun to increasingly recognize the necessity of learning how to market their practices to managed care companies.

This book will tell you how! We will focus on the managed care companies you are particularly interested in—the preferred provider networks, since those are the managed care organizations that contract with private practice therapists. And we will concentrate upon strategies that will help you to hone in on the higher quality networks.

At the present time, there are three interrelated challenges to therapists who want to market themselves to managed care organizations:

1. Getting accepted on lists of preferred psychotherapist providers with managed care organizations.
2. Generating a flow of patient referrals once the therapist is accepted onto panels of preferred providers. (This does not usually occur automatically.)
3. Retention on active referral panels over the long term. This means surviving cuts in therapist-provider lists which usually occur around the second year after major contracts are signed.

Chapters 2 through 5 of this book will help the therapist develop strategies for meeting the above challenges.

Marketing does not occur in a vacuum. Therefore, I will address two attitudinal issues that often impair therapists' ability to market successfully to managed care companies. Chapter 1 will address the therapist's perception of managed care, managed care companies, and the new behavioral health care marketplace. Chapter 8 will help therapists see themselves as marketers—and feel professional and ethical about that.

Marketing effectiveness is measured by the quality of the results. If one signs many contracts that produce very little income or put the therapist at great legal risk, the marketing effort has been counterproductive. Strategic marketing that targets particular managed care organizations and/or contracts is necessary to ensure the therapist's satisfaction with the end result. Chapter 6 will cover strategic marketing.

Effective marketing also requires understanding the marketplace. But the marketplace in behavioral health care is dynamic and creative. The chances are that the structures of behavioral health care delivery will be substantially changed in two to five years. Most businesses, including therapy businesses, find it useful to market with at least a two-year perspective. That means recognizing and understanding trends in the marketplace. Chapter 7 will provide a framework for understanding these trends.

The marketplace is not the only change agent for the behavioral health care delivery industry. Just as managed care was originated by corporations and insurance companies to contain costs, now managed competition is under development by the federal government to contain costs again. As this book goes to press proposals are under development by the Clinton administration that will impact the behavioral health care delivery system anew. In Chapter 8 we will discuss the probable direction of those changes and the impact they will probably have on your practice.

One can get all of the tips on marketing and then feel overwhelmed, not knowing what to do first. This is especially true of therapists—folks who often see themselves as being talented in ways that are not business-related. So Chapter 9 will speak to how business-related your practice probably already is, especially regarding quality-based marketing. This should reduce any cognitive dissonance you might experience regarding marketing, and help you base your personal marketing efforts on the strengths which probably already exist in your practice. Chapter 10 will then provide tools for designing a marketing plan and the steps for implementing that plan. It also includes a number of places for you to do your own worksheets, based upon information from the rest of the book. It is my hope and expectation that by reading this book and completing the worksheets you can design a step-by-step marketing plan that fits you personally, while marketing your practice to managed care companies and helping you thrive under managed competition when the American Health Security Act comes into effect.

NOTES

1. From private communication by Alex R. Rodriguez, M.D. on 6-10-93.
2. *Employee Benefit News*, August 1992, edition, Page 4.
3. *Managed Care Strategies Newsletter*, September, 1992, Page 8.
4. *Psychotherapy Finances Survey Report*, Volume 17, No 12, 1992, page 1.
5. *Open Minds Newsletter*, June, 1992, Volume 5, Issue 3.
6. *Managed Care Strategies* Newsletter. Volume 1, Number 1, September, 1992. Page 10.

1/
Coming to Terms with Managed Care

Throughout America business is in turmoil. Therapists see ample evidence of this as we observe the increasing numbers of clients arriving in our offices with work-related stress problems. These same market forces are now impacting behavioral health (mental health and chemical dependency) care delivery. And the form of this upheaval in the behavioral health care industry is managed care. Corporate America is meeting global competition by reorganizing itself and downsizing. Through managed care, behavioral health care delivery systems are reorganizing and downsizing.

Coming to terms with managed care is not just the concern of this chapter; it is really what this whole book is about. Finding ways to make managed care work so that psychotherapist providers and their clients can survive and thrive is the overall goal, a goal whose first step is marketing. But this is an interdependent task, because marketing itself is at least partly dependent upon feeling good about the customer. Most marketers will tell you that the better the feelings you can have about your customers, the more effective your marketing will be. And managed care companies are the marketing customers for the therapists who will read this book. So, coming to terms with managed care is also a desirable precursor to marketing to managed care.

I believe that coming to terms with managed care requires that the therapist go through three somewhat interrelated processes:

1. Psychological
   We must adjust to the loss of indemnity insurance as the predominant behavioral health care payment system. Accompanying that is the loss of the relatively unsupervised and benign professional practices which were possible under indemnity insurance. We need to process the feelings connected with sudden adjustment to a radically new professional environment.

2. Educational

   Understanding managed care within its historic, business, and especially its economic context should make it possible to view this new system as a needed change in which the therapist has a necessary and central part to play.

3. Empowering

   As we come to adjust to and understand managed care, it is important that we begin to find ways of moving from a passive, reactive position in which we feel helpless to find mechanisms for constructive initiative to begin to make managed care work for our patients and ourselves. Marketing can be the first part of that process.

PSYCHOLOGICAL ADJUSTMENT

Most therapists have come to an experience of managed care only recently and it has seemed to come out of nowhere to decimate our practices and severely complicate the delivery of mental health services. Psychological adjustment to this change is necessary for us to effectively market to managed care companies. Three areas of psychological adjustment are called for: 1. crisis work to deal with sudden change, 2. accommodation to an altered professional identity, and 3. loss adjustment.

1. Sudden Change: Crises

We are experiencing our own variant of crisis and reacting in various intensities with the same responses our clients utilize to react to crisis. The Chinese ideograph for crisis consists of two symbols: one for danger and the other for opportunity.[1] In a crisis, the balance of equilibrium becomes upset and one tends to become overwhelmed with anxiety.[2] Support, education, and adaptive behavior are the tools for coping; when these are insufficient or not forthcoming quickly enough, one begins to feel helpless.[3] If you are among those who have begun to feel helpless, I hope that this book will provide the education that will make it possible for you to turn this particular danger into opportunity. And I hope that you will use marketing as one of your primary adaptive behaviors. As you know, any concrete steps — such as reading this book — can constitute adaptive behavior and can begin the process of coming out of helplessness.

2. Altered Professional Identity

Managed care means that we are moving from a professional self-identity as independent practitioners to becoming subcontractors for insurance surrogate companies. When looking at this change, Dr. Claire V. Wilson, who at that time was a regional director for U.S. Behavioral Health of California, Inc., called psychotherapy, "The last cottage industry."[4] Others have recognized our profession with the same analogy,[5] noting that indemnity reimbursement and training patterns resulted in many therapists operating out of offices within or adjacent to our own homes (including the author). This arrangement included supervision only on a discretionary basis.

While many of us engaged in extensive postgraduate educational efforts through the numerous offerings and books constantly being generated in our field, in most cases this was also voluntary and some in the field undertook little or no postgraduate education at all. Large numbers of therapists worked very hard to develop increasingly effective treatments, but the experimental literature continued to demonstrate no statistically significant differences in effectiveness between one form of therapy and another. Employee Assistance Professionals developed and publicized medical offset studies which demonstrated cost savings over time. But these studies focused primarily upon chemical dependency and inpatient therapy. And corporate benefit managers began to question the statistical validity measures and to increasingly find the conclusions irrelevant, as they had to focus upon short-term goals of reducing the large behavioral health care cost increases that were devastating corporate financial departments.

In the meantime consumers (clients, insurance companies, and corporations) were unable to find easily-available indexes by which to differentiate variances in therapist quality. For all of these reasons, managed care companies found a ready audience when they offered to manage behavioral health care. Thus our industry is rapidly changing to one in which our work is increasingly monitored, we find ourselves pressured to become parts of treatment teams instead of individual practitioners, and others have substantial input about the quantity and quality of the treatment we render.

These changes mimic similar ones that managed care brought to medical health care practitioners a few years ago; like physicians, we are often reacting with anger as well as a justified sense of diminished value and of powerlessness.

3. Loss

Even as we have coped with crisis and the redefinition of our professional identity, a parallel process has also occurred: loss adjustment. Most of us have experienced managed care primarily as a loss. The most obvious part of that loss is the extreme erosion of the old indemnity insurance plans[6] as managed care has grown to replace them, with the numerous changes this involves. As indicated above, the erosion of our freedom to practice with the kind of independence that accompanied indemnity insurance constitutes one of the primary losses.

Nearly all of us have reacted to those losses with stages of loss adjustment that are academically familiar to us: denial, bargaining, anger, acknowledgement, and, finally, acceptance. Let us elaborate on each of these:

Denial

Most therapists have experienced at least some denial. And some therapists have continued to cling to denial, still saying that managed care will not become really important in their particular geographic region. Some regions still exist where it is not well established. But managed care companies are rapidly expanding all over the United States now. Or we imagine that national health care may replace managed care. That may be true, but most of the national health care proposals are built around expansions of the present system.

Bargaining

We continue to bargain, hoping that in some way we can structure our practices to accept only fee-for-service or non-managed-care-reimbursed clients. Some therapists have been successful at this, but the statistics suggest that they are increasingly in the minority among those who are in practice on a full-time basis.

Anger

We all know that anger is an appropriate adjustment to loss, and most of us have experienced it with managed care. Beyond that, the policies of some of the managed care companies have generated enormous anger on the part of therapists not only for ourselves but also for our clients. And this anger is only gradually getting worked through.

Acknowledgement

Probably most therapists have come to a somewhat reluctant acknowledgement of managed care as a primary, if not dominant, force in behavioral health care delivery, but that is still somewhat grudging.

Acceptance

Finally, many therapists are, each of us individually in our own ways, coming to an acceptance of managed care.

This acceptance is necessary because some form of acceptance is required before therapists can begin to operate within the system to truly participate in managed care, have a voice in the field, and make constructive contributions to it. But acceptance needs to mean more than just the last stage of a loss-adjustment process in which we make a psychological accommodation to the near-total replacement of indemnity insurance by managed care. It needs to also acknowledge what managed care is.

EDUCATIONAL ADJUSTMENT

Understanding what managed care truly is involves seeing it within an important historic and economic context. That is fortunate, because, as noted above, this kind of contextual understanding can result in a small, but very important, cognitive shift. This cognitive shift is valuable because it can generate better feelings toward managed care so that a solid emotional framework for marketing can be constructed. I hope that an understanding of the historic and economic context will help you move from perceiving managed care as a problem (which appears to be the perception of most therapists) to seeing it as a solution. That change should make it possible to feel differently about marketing to managed care. Instead of feeling that you are consorting with the enemy, you can recognize that you are contributing to making the new mechanisms for behavioral health care delivery work effectively, professionally, and ethically. For most therapists, a shift of this kind is a necessary precursor to ethical marketing.

Managed care has grown directly out of America's crisis in health care financing. Nearly everyone is aware of the tremendous annual health care increases over the past decade. There are high costs to continuing these annual health care increases, with America's health care bill reaching some $800 billion in 1992[7] and average monthly insurance premiums reaching $101.00 for families and $35.00 for individuals.[8] But the highest payers are American businesses, who usually pay around 60% while employees pay around 40% of health care costs.[9]

This situation has had a profound impact upon corporate profits and competitiveness, so much so that in the early 1980s corporate chief executive officers began strongly pressuring their benefit managers to do something about cost containment. Managed care companies responded by offering cost containment through (1) contracting with providers at reduced rates, and (2) managing health care to reduce costs.

On a company-by-company basis they were fairly successful in reducing the escalation of these expenses. But just when medical health care cost increases began to level off, corporate financial officers began to notice something that looked like a cost shift. As medical health care cost increases de-escalated, a corresponding escalation began to occur in behavioral health care costs. In the mid to late 1980s, behavioral health care cost increases began to register in double digits—up to 27% in 1987.[10] More than 95% of corporate benefit managers surveyed reported extensive increases in both utilization and costs associated with behavioral health care, while nearly 11% of the nation's health care expenditures were spent on mental illness in 1989.[11] Honeywell Inc. reported in 1988 that mental disorders were number two on its list of the top five conditions leading to total annual individual claims of more than $10,000.00.[12]

Corporations began to consider drastic responses to this behavioral health care cost escalation. The responses generally fell into two categories: drop behavioral health coverage altogether or contract for behavioral health through managed care with the hope of substantial cost containment. In a 1989 survey of 400 corporate executives from companies representing 3.9

million workers, more than half of the respondents foresaw restricting or excluding coverage for dependents' mental health or chemical-dependency illnesses.[13]

Various business surveys indicate that when confronted with the choice between dropping behavioral health coverage or contracting for managed care, numerous businesses chose to contract with managed care. The number of companies offering behavioral managed care programs grew from "fewer than a dozen" to hundreds between 1985 and 1992.[14] And by August, 1992 it was estimated that 90% of employers had moved into managed care at least to some degree.[15]

It is important to note that the choice considered by employers was between managed care and dropping behavioral health coverage, not between managed care and indemnity insurance. Indemnity insurance was seen as the vehicle that brought the unsustainable cost increases.

As psychotherapists, we are used to indemnity insurance, which has carried many comparable benefits for us. So we have a natural inclination to compare managed care to indemnity insurance and prefer indemnity by a wide margin. But the above statistics indicate that corporate America has experienced indemnity insurance as too expensive and has opted for managed care in lieu of dropping behavioral health coverage altogether. The marketplace is saying to us that the choice we want to make—between managed care and indemnity—is not available. The real choice is between managed care and no behavioral health coverage. Given that option, managed care suddenly takes on a different character. Instead of being the problem choice in the decision between managed care and indemnity, it is the solution choice in the decision between managed care and no behavioral health coverage.

I believe that it makes sense to shift our perception from seeing managed care as a problem to seeing it as the beginning of a solution. It is a beginning solution to the continuance of behavioral health care within a financially constrained marketplace.

EMPOWERING

If you can make this cognitive shift of coming to see managed care as the beginning of a solution to the preservation of employer-sponsored behavioral health care, that concept can become the conceptual framework for repositioning your practice. It can constitute the first step in marketing your practice to managed care. And if you market to managed care creatively (see below), you can position yourself to pick your managed care partners.

It makes sense to recognize that your practice will be part of a vertical delivery system. This system consists of: 1. the employer deciding what kind of behavioral health benefits will be offered and 2. purchasing them from a managed care company that 3. contracts for the services from you, the therapist-provider. Utilizing a case manager, the M.C.O. both supervises and consults with you to ensure effective treatment. That consultative mechanism generates reports from the provider to the managed care company regarding treatment effectiveness and utilization requests. Periodically, the managed care company in turn reports back to the corporation with summaries of utilization, cost, and effectiveness. Thus, this system includes a financing flow from employer to provider when contracting for care and it also includes a reporting flow from provider to employer when reporting results.

Since this new delivery system constitutes a treatment financing team, your marketing should focus on a goal of selecting quality managed care organizations as your team partners. The near-term marketplace realities may leave you little room to make choices regarding your M.C.O. teammates, but it still makes sense to hold that concept as a long-term goal.

We all know from motivational literature that setting a goal and then creating a clear vision of it provide an extra psychological boost for getting to the goal, even when the goal initially seems far away. Since therapists all have a background of eight to ten years of schooling and internship before licensure, this far-term goal-setting is familiar to us.

But the goal-setting needs to occur within a context. Once you come to the concept of managed care as a solution, I encourage you to use that acceptance to consider how you want to reposition your practice within managed care, formulate a goal, and then visualize that goal.

The current behavioral health care marketplace is dynamic, extremely competitive for managed care companies, and rife with opportunities for proactive psychotherapists. If you create a niche that helps M.C.O.s compete in their own markets, you will be highly valued. This can bring you enough managed care contracts so that you can begin to pick and choose which M.C.O.s you want as your partners.

Economists and stock market traders can attest to the fact that dramatic economic changes nearly always bring multiple opportunities. Dramatic changes have just hit the behavioral health care delivery field, beginning with a huge increase in the number of M.C.O.s. Now, the field is beginning to stratify and market niches are being developed among managed care companies. Such an arena is a gold mine for those who know how to market with innovative ideas and services. While M.C.O.s are seeking their market niches, this is a time when the individual practitioner can creatively develop and market his or her own niche. In this way you can position yourself to appeal to those compatible managed care companies that you feel will make good partners for you.

The initial rationale for managed care was cost containment. Many M.C.O.s have now developed to meet that need and they all tend to meet it relatively equally well. At this point, intense competition between managed care companies is beginning to develop and the M.C.O.s are experiencing a need to differentiate themselves through offering something unique to potential corporate clients. They are starting to opt for such market niches as very low cost, very high quality, or unique (and needed) services. Any therapist who can bring them a market niche advantage in this positioning process will be highly valued.

What this means is that the therapist should proactively and creatively develop service or practice qualities that are needed and valued by M.C.O. marketing departments or M.C.O. managements. They fall into two categories: those that will help the managed care company to market itself and those that will help the M.C.O. become more internally effective in its present functioning so that present marketing directions will become more competitive. Examples of such service or practice qualities might be: conducting therapy in sign language, compliance enhancement, offering services that enhance patients' capabilities at work (since employers are the M.C.O.'s clients), providing services that are uniquely valued by employees who want therapists who understand their lifestyle (such as born-again Christians or gays or lesbians), rebates for clients who relapse, well-validated quality assurance statistics, or traditional services enhanced by the teaching of future problem-prevention skills at no additional cost.

In order to offer such services, the therapist must first understand what is needed. And understanding what is needed means getting into and operating within the managed care system enough to recognize how it functions, where it is going, what end purchasers are requesting, and where problems exist. This global perspective should result in the therapist developing an understanding of where the opportunities are.

Below (Fig. 1) you will find seven building blocks that, together, constitute a stairway to success with managed care. There is a wide range of service delivery options opening up for the 1990s. Within this rainbow of options are many niches that are potentially available for you to utilize. I encourage you to climb this stairway of understanding of managed care and develop your quality and market niche. In this way, you can position yourself within that rainbow of service delivery options and get the financial reward at the end of this new rainbow.

Figure 1: Stairway to Success

Following are the steps in the stairway to success within the rainbow of service delivery options in the 90s:

1. Accept managed care. This means accepting on a personal level that you are willing to work with this new behavioral health care delivery mechanism. What is required here is a global acceptance of the concept in principle, not an acceptance of every managed care company's policies.
2. Join managed care. Become a preferred provider for at least a couple of managed care companies.
3. Develop both a global and in-depth knowledge of the managed care industry to understand trends, needs, and opportunities.
4. Develop a service, skill, or practice quality that could help a managed care company enhance its marketplace competitive position.
5. Package the service, skill, or practice quality in such a way that you can communicate its advantages to the managed care company—especially to the M.C.O.'s marketing team.
6. Investigate a large number of managed care companies sufficiently to discover which would be interested in your unique package.
7. Market your package to the most appropriate managed care companies.

SUMMARY

In this first chapter we have considered the first step in the above outline: coming to some form of acceptance of managed care. As you consider step two, "Joining managed care," you may be saying to yourself something like, "I would love to join managed care. However, each time I approach a managed care organization, they tell me their provider networks are full. I feel I have come to some acceptance of them, but they have not come to accept me."

That situation is what marketing is all about. The initial challenge for most private practice psychotherapists is to get on preferred provider panels. In the next chapter, we will discuss finding and contracting with managed care organizations (M.C.O.s) that have openings on their preferred provider lists. In the chapter after that (Chapter 3) we will look at breaking into M.C.O.s that have officially closed their provider panels.

NOTES

1. Aguilera, Donna and Messick, Janice. *Crisis Intervention Therapy for Psychological Emergencies.* St. Louis: C. V. Mosby Company, 1982, page 1.
2. Ibid. Pages 1–12.
3. Ibid. Pages 1–32.
4. Personal communication in July, 1991 from Claire V. (Ginger) Wilson, Ph.D., who has had a variety of positions with managed care including vice president of development for Mustard Seed, Inc. and southern California regional director for U.S. Behavioral Health/Travelers.
5. Practice Directorate Workbook compiled for the August, 1992 convention of the American Psychological Association.
6. Up to a 50% drop by 1995 by one estimate. *Managed Care Strategies Newsletter,* September, 1992, page 8.
7. *Los Angeles Daily News* Newspaper, page 3, for 7-12-92.
8. *Los Angeles Times* Newspaper for 08-30-92 Business Section (D), page 1.
9. Ibid.
10. Foster Higgins 1988, 89, and 91 Benefit Surveys.
11. Reprinted from BUSINESS & HEALTH, December, 1989. Copyright 1980 and published by Medical Economics Publishing Inc., Montvale, N.J. 07645-1742. All rights reserved. None of the content of this publication may be reproduced, stored in a retrieval system or transmitted in any form or by any means (electronic, mechanical, photocopying, recording or otherwise) without the prior written permission of the publisher.
12. Ibid.
13. Ibid.
14. *Employee Assistance Magazine.* February, 1992. Vol. 4. No. 7, article "Managing Treatment" page 7.
15. *Employee Benefit News.* August 1992 edition. Page 4.

2/
The First Marketing Challenge: Finding Open Managed Care Panels

Psychotherapists face three interrelated challenges to marketing their practices to managed care companies: (1) inclusion on preferred provider lists, (2) referrals of clients, and (3) long-term retention on preferred provider lists.

CONTRACTING CYCLES

Managed care organizations (M.C.O.s) tend to expand in phases. In one of these phases, which we will call the Provider Expansion Phase, the M.C.O. is especially interested in contracting with new psychotherapist providers. In all of the other phases of their business expansion cycle, M.C.O.s are relatively uninterested in contracting with new psychotherapists because their provider panels are full. But most psychotherapists become aware of new M.C.O.s operating in their local area some time after the provider expansion phase, and therefore find themselves "locked out" of participation. So, obtaining preferred provider status on managed care company lists can be seen as primarily a matter of timing. The cycle is shown in Figure 2.

When a corporation or employee group decides to contract with a managed care company, it calls for bids. Once M.C.O.s submit bids, they are compared on various criteria. Usually, the most important issue is

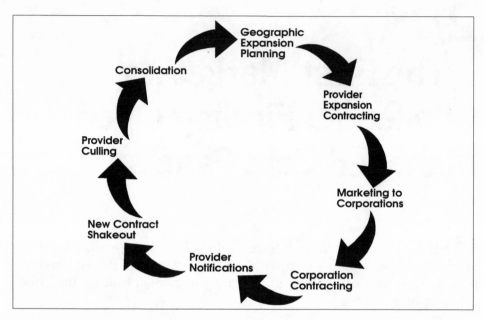

Figure 2: M.C.O. Contracting Cycle

cost, followed closely by the ability to service the contract. M.C.O.s generally feel that they have a competitive edge if they can promise extensive coverage for all of the firm's employees. But to truly service the contract— to put substance behind the service promise—requires that the M.C.O. demonstrate a previously contracted psychotherapist provider network. And that network should evidence substantial quantity and quality, as well as geographic dispersion. Thus, the service promise which is inherent in contract bids requires the M.C.O. to engage in extensive provider recruitment. And the provider recruitment (expansion) phase of the business development cycle must occur before the corporate contract development phase of the cycle in order to ensure that the M.C.O.'s bids will be competitive.

In some states, such as California, state regulations require managed care organizations to demonstrate a previously contracted, geographically dispersed provider network before the managed care organization will be allowed to become fully operative. This means that the managed care organization must demonstrate a network of previously contracted providers within certain small distances of every employee, dependent, and retiree of each corporation the M.C.O. intends to do business with.

To summarize: most provider networks must be developed prior to the corporate marketing phase because (1) contracting employers will prefer to do business only with managed care organizations that have an extensive and well-documented network in place, and/or (2) the state regulations mandate provider network completion prior to providing permission to become fully operative. This clarifies why the managed care organization's provider development phase constitutes its one period of intense provider recruiting. This provider expansion effort is the easiest time for psychotherapists to contract with managed care organizations, because at this point the M.C.O.s have an extremely strong incentive to complete those contracts in an expeditious manner.

The primary difficulty for psychotherapist-providers at this stage is finding the M.C.O.s. Typically, psychotherapists discover new M.C.O.s when those organizations notify providers that current patients are now covered under a new insurance contract. That notification occurs only after the managed care organization has been chosen by an employer and has begun to service the new contract. However, the notification period can be as much as one year or more after the pre-marketing (provider-contracting) phase has been completed!

In most cases, when a managed care organization develops its regional provider network, it oversubscribes the network. That is, the M.C.O. contracts with far more psychotherapist providers than they can anticipate ever needing in order to genuinely service the employer contracts they may obtain in the foreseeable future. This is usually done for marketing reasons. All other things being equal, an employer might be much more interested in a bid from a managed care organization that has a contracted provider network of 1,000 local therapists than one that has a provider network of 500 local therapists—even when a network of only 250 therapists would be more than sufficient to fully service the contract.

Since provider networks are often substantially oversubscribed during the expansion phase, psychotherapists who do not discover a managed care organization until its notification phase are usually unable to get into the network. Therefore, therapists who wish to market their practices to M.C.O.s must develop ways of discovering new or expanding M.C.O.s when those organizations are in their provider contracting phase for the therapist's geographic area. This may take some considerable time and energy, but it is time and energy well spent because the provider contracting phase of the M.C.O.'s expansion cycle is the most productive time for the psychotherapist to obtain preferred provider panel credentialling.

You should also consider your initial efforts to find expansion-phase M.C.O.s as just the first step of an ongoing process that will continue for the foreseeable future in your long-term marketing strategy (Chapter 10). Once you have found and contracted with an initial group of expansion-phase M.C.O.s, you should continue that process with additional companies. The M.C.O.s that hold contracts with employers in your geographic area keep those contracts for only a relatively short period—usually around two years. At the end of the initial contract period, they are renegotiated. And often the new contracts are with different M.C.O.s. So you should realize that the employees who are locked into a contract that allows them to see you under a particular managed care company may become locked into different preferred provider networks in the future if their present M.C.O. is displaced in favor of a different one when the corporate contract comes up for renewal. Because of this, you should initiate an ongoing program to discover new M.C.O.s when they expand to your area. In this way, you can contract with all of the potential managed care players in your area and increase the odds of being a preferred provider for any M.C.O. that wins the contract renewal of your area's employers.

FINDING EXPANSION-PHASE M.C.O.s

One would think that finding expansion phase managed care companies would be a relatively simple matter of just obtaining lists of those organizations and then contacting them. That is not the case. Such lists are extremely difficult to obtain since there is no one good central clearing house that M.C.O.s have agreed to utilize, state insurance boards are usually not equipped to compile or disseminate such lists, and the information is constantly changing. In the remainder of this chapter we will discuss ways to obtain information about M.C.O.s that have open lists. This can be done through:

1. Professional organizations,
2. Publications,
3. Behavioral health hospital marketing departments,
4. Consultants,
5. List development companies,
6. Marketing companies, and
7. Networking.

1. Professional Organizations

One of the best ways of finding expansion-phase managed care companies is through therapists' national professional organizations. Some of these organizations maintain lists of therapists who have met especially rigid requirements, including post-licensure experience and national testing. Two of the national professional organizations publish these lists in national directories and actively market to both established and emerging M.C.O.s on behalf of their registrants.

Clinical Psychologists

Psychologists can apply for listing in the "National Registry of Providers in Psychology" by applying to the Council for National Register of Health Service Providers at 1730 Rhode Island Ave., Washington, D.C. [Phone: (202) 833-2377].

Psychologists should also connect with the Practice Directorate of the American Psychological Association at 750 First Street, N.E., Washington, D.C. 20002-4242 [Phone: (202) 336-5500]. This organization is seeking to market psychologist members in managed behavioral health care delivery through direct contracting with employers. Although the Practice Directorate does not directly aid members in obtaining insurance-based managed care contracts, it is in a position to provide extensive information and support to that effort.

Clinical Social Workers

Clinical social workers can apply to the American Board of Examiners in Clinical Social Work to become Board Certified Diplomates in clinical social work, which will allow them to be listed in the "American Board of Examiners Directory" and the ABEnet computer network. The American Board of Examiners in Clinical Social Work is located at 8484 Georgia Avenue, Suite 800, Silver Spring, Md. 20910-5604 [Phone: (301) 587-8783]. The American Board goes a step beyond publishing a national directory through providing a computer listing which managed care companies can access through modem hookups.

Inclusion in the National Registry of Providers in Psychology or the directory of the American Board of Examiners in Clinical Social Work is especially important for therapists who wish to contract with a managed care organization during the M.C.O.'s pre-marketing (provider contracting) business phase. This is because managed care organizations have very high incentives to utilize the national organizations' lists when they move into a new market. Sophisticated M.C.O.s utilize the national professional organizations' lists because:

1. The professional organizations have pre-screened the quality of the providers (eliminating — or at least simplifying — that need for the managed care organization),
2. The M.C.O. can hone their provider-contracting mailings to specific geographic areas by utilizing the information in the professional organizations' lists, and
3. The lists are up-to-date regarding addresses, specialties, and malpractice insurance coverage. These three advantages can result in great cost and time savings for the managed care organizations that use national directories.

Psychiatrists

The American Psychiatric Association publishes a biographical directory through their Office of Survey Designs and Analysis. But, according to Ruth Yoshpe, M.P.H., health economist with the American Psychiatric Association's Office of Economic Affairs' Committee on Managed Care, the directory is alphabetical and not listed by geography or specialty (though special geographic or specialty computer runs could be obtained should a managed care organization request it). She notes that the American Psychiatric Association suggests a different route for contact with expansion-phase managed care companies. When an M.C.O. moves into a new geographic region, the A.M.A.'s local district is encouraged to set up a face-to-face dialogue on the managed care company's criteria for provider selection, triage, medical necessity, and referral patterns.[1] Ms. Yoshpe notes that most psychiatrists tend to affiliate with managed care organizations through psychiatrist-run Independent Practice Associations, Preferred Provider Organizations, or Exclusive Provider Organizations. (Please see Chapter 7 for a fuller understanding of I.P.A.s, P.P.O.s, and E.P.O.s.) Information about the biographical directory or their component book which lists district branches can be obtained through the American Psychiatric Association, 1400 K Street N.W., Washington, D.C. 20005 [Phone: (202) 682-6000]. Psychiatrists should also consider affiliating with the National Association of Managed Care Physicians and the American Society of Addiction Medicine. You will probably find it very helpful to become certified by the American Society of Addiction Medicine as well.

Marriage and Family Therapists

The national professional organization for marriage and family therapists is the American Association of Marriage and Family Therapy, located at 1100 17th Street, N.W., 10th floor, Washington, D.C. 20036-4601 [Phone: (202) 452-0109]. Lizabet M. Boroughs, who is with the Professional Practice Department of the AAMFT, has provided the following information: "AAMFT Clinical Members must meet rigorous standards regarding academic training and supervised clinical experience. These standards established by AAMFT have been adopted by many states in their licensing requirements for marriage and family therapists. Currently 30 states license or certify marriage and family therapists. AAMFT is working hard to ensure that health care reform (see Chapter 8) includes comprehensive mental health care services including marriage and family therapy. As part of its health care reform efforts, AAMFT is educating managed care companies that MFTs offer a variety of high-quality, cost-effective, solution-oriented mental health services. MFTs should join AAMFT to ensure that their services are included in the changing health care delivery system as well as to enhance their individual marketing program."[2]

It is also important for marriage and family therapists to connect with their state organization for marketing on a local geographic basis. Usually, the vendorship committee is the appropriate group within the state to connect with. Many state organizations contact managed care companies all over the country without regard for state boundaries, since they are seeking to help their in-state members with out-of-state contracts.

2. Publications

Another good method for keeping current with the emergence of new M.C.O.s into the therapist's local area is through keeping abreast of publications that contain information on this subject. In the last few years some specialty newsletters directed specifically to behavioral managed care have emerged. The following are probably the most well established:

Psychotherapy Finances
c/o Ridgewood Financial Institute, Inc.
1016 Clemons Street, Suite 407
Jupiter, Fla. 33477

The editor of Psychotherapy Finances is Gayle Tuttle, who is very concerned about what happens to individual psychotherapy providers in the behavioral health care marketplace. This newsletter usually has a section entitled "Managed Care Alert: New Opportunities for Providers" which highlights M.C.O.s that are in an expansion-contracting phase with psychotherapist providers. Psychotherapy Finances also usually runs a section on practice building.

Open Minds—The Behavioral
Health Industry Analyst
4465 Old Harrisburg Road
Gettysburg, Pa. 17325

Open Minds is published primarily by Monica Oss. Ms. Oss has made it a point to do substantial research on behavioral managed care organizations and then to make that information available to her clients, so this is a research-oriented newsletter which can alert you to trends in the industry. Her newsletter usually profiles one behavioral health care company in each issue and she tries to keep her readers current regarding new contract awards. This information tends to refer to major awards on at least a statewide or regional scope, rather than local contract awards, however.

Mental Health Weekly
Manisses Communications Group, Inc.
P.O. Box 3357
Providence, R.I. 02906-0757

It is not unusual for this weekly newsletter to devote as much as a third of its space to managed care information, often referring to developments that imply openings for new psychotherapy providers.

Since the specialty newsletters for behavioral managed care are still fairly new and somewhat limited because of their newsletter format, it can be useful for you to supplement your reading with publications in related areas. Managed care organizations also must sell their product. And the purchasers of behavioral managed care products are usually benefits managers. Therefore, it is useful to subscribe to one of the publications that address themselves to benefits managers. Two of those publications are:

Employee Benefit News
P.O. Box 7389
Marietta, Ga. 30065

Managed Care Outlook
1101 King Street
P.O. Box 1453
Alexandria, Va. 22313

An additional publication to consider is:

Benefits Today
The Bureau of National Affairs, Inc.
Washington, D.C. 20037

Published by the federal government, it covers industry trends and governmental regulations and reviews special reports that touch directly on behavioral managed care directions. While rarely listing specific managed care company expansions, it does give useful information about responses to federal regulations, including the federal managed care programs of champus and medicare. As managed competition has emerged this newsletter has become especially valuable, since it is current and authoritative on federal governmental developments. It will probably become even more useful as the American Health Security Act enters its implementation phase.

One of the precursors of behavioral managed care was the employee assistance field. A number of employee assistance companies reformulated themselves into behavioral managed care companies, many of whose executives and staff employees were employee assistance professionals. Thus, reading E.A.P. journals will keep you abreast of changes in managed care and will often alert you to new M.C.O.s that are expanding to your local area. The two publications you will probably find most useful in this field are:

E.A.P. Digest
Performance Resource Press
1863 Technology Drive
Troy, Mich. 48083-4244

Employee Assistance
P.O. Box 2604
Waco, Tex.
76204-2604

There is one more group of publications that is useful in keeping current on the managed care organizations that are expanding into the therapist's local area: the business press. Maurie Cullen, a clinical social worker provider and nationally recognized consultant on managed care, states, "Psychotherapists must recognize that they are small business owners and therefore they must keep up with both local business news and national publications such as the *Wall Street Journal*."[3] A publication such as the *Journal* or *Barrons* can be helpful in keeping track of macro changes in the managed care field. Major insurance companies are continuously purchasing managed care organizations, merging M.C.O.s, developing new M.C.O. products, and expanding to new geographic markets. Health care stocks have already become much more volatile as they have reacted to managed competition. Major changes in both ownership and structure of M.C.O.s can be expected as managed competition gets integrated into the marketplace. And there is every likelihood of a series of well-funded new insurance products that will be developed in response to the American Health Security Act. Carefully looking for these developments can alert the clinician to managed care expansions, splits, and consolidations in his or her local area.

In light of these probable changes, an additional group of publications you might want to consider consists of corporate annual reports and other information sent to stockholders. Purchasing even a few shares of the insurance company stock can entitle you to receive information from the major insurance company investors in the behavioral health care area. This information will also help you to keep ahead of some of the trends in the industry. (See Chapter 7.)

You might also want to consider the following:

Additional Sources of Managed Care Information

1994 National Directory of Managed Care Companies and Employee Assistance Programs Professional Health Plan 5856 College Avenue, Suite 206 Oakland, Calif. 94618 (800) 428-7559	*Business Insurance* (weekly) Crain Communications 740 Rush Street Chicago, Ill. 60611-2590 (800) 678-9595
AMCRA Monitor (ten issues annually) American Managed Care and Review Association 1227 25th Street, N.W., Suite 610 Washington, D.C. 20037	*Managed Care Week* (weekly) Atlantic Information Services, Inc. 1050 17th Street, N.W., Suite 480 Washington, D.C. 20036 (800) 521-4323
Behavioral Healthcare Tomorrow Journal Institute for Behavioral Healthcare 1110 MarWest Street, Suite E Tiburon, Calif. 94920	*Managed Healthcare News* (monthly) P.O. Box 10460 Eugene, Oreg. 97440

Since subscribing to a number of publications can be costly, my suggestion is that the reader contact a number of different publishers and ask for sample copies. It will then be easier to make an informed choice regarding which publications meet your needs best. Another way to handle the cost is to work with a group of colleagues. You can each subscribe to one or two journals or newsletters and get together regularly to share information gleaned from them. This is just one of a number of advantages to the use of small colleague groups as a support network when you are marketing to managed care companies. Generally, you will find that most of the marketing suggestions in this book will be easier to implement if you form a marketing support group with colleagues.

3. Behavioral Health Hospital Marketing Departments

You will probably find that private mental health and/or chemical dependency hospitals in your local area will be particularly good resources for finding managed care companies that are in their provider contracting expansion phase. Most behavioral health hospitals have invested heavily in their marketing staffs. If you are open to obtaining staff privileges at the hospital—thus indicating that you are open to hospitalizing patients there—the hospital marketing staff will often provide lists of the managed care organizations with which they are negotiating. These hospitals have a substantial need to find and contract with M.C.O.s during their expansion phase, so they tend to locate the new M.C.O.s early.

Some large national hospital chains are also beginning to develop their own managed care products, including preferred provider organizations. This is a way for them to expand into the local community to deliver outpatient services and then to link those outpatient services to the hospital, so that any connected inpatient services are locked into the hospital which is driving the outpatient product. Hospital administrators are often in charge of these product lines and they tend to pick locally active therapists to be on their networks—especially if those therapists have already established a pattern of referring to their hospital.

4. Consultants

Managed care consultants can be a good source of information about all phases of marketing to managed care, including how to find expansion-phase companies. Three of the national consultants are:

Michael A. Freeman, M.D.
c/o Behavioral Health Alliance
1110 MarWest Street, Suite E
Tiburon, Calif. 94920

Monica Oss
4465 Old Harrisburg Road
Gettysburg, Pa. 17325

Maurie Cullen, M.S.W., B.C.D.
16255 Ventura Boulevard, Suite 806
Encino, Calif. 91316

National consultants are sometimes rather expensive, but local consultants can be quite reasonable. It is always necessary to check out how knowledgeable a consultant really is about behavioral managed care. Often, consultants who know managed care well have specialized in medical managed care, so their knowledge of behavioral M.C.O.s is somewhat deficient. One way to get a clue about this is to just look at who is speaking or writing about managed care in your local area. Or ask colleagues about who seems to be knowledgeable in this area. Even when that person does not identify himself or herself as a consultant, if you offer a consulting fee, you may find that he or she will be willing to work with you and may provide extremely valuable suggestions.

If you decide to utilize a consultant, you should first develop your own goals and tentative marketing plan (see Chapter 10). This will help you decide how you want to use a consultant. Before contacting a consultant, write down how much you can afford to spend, what you want, what your goals are, and what time periods you envision for accomplishing those goals. By making those decisions, even on a tentative basis, you can minimize the time you spend with a consultant (reducing costs since they generally charge on a time basis) and you can make a more informed decision regarding whether or not a given consultant fits that framework well.

If you anticipate utilizing a consultant over a period of time, see if he or she will agree to an initial appointment on a reduced fee basis so that you can mutually decide whether you will work well together. Before asking for this, let the consultant know that you anticipate a long-term relationship (even if it will be intermittent), since a reduced fee is rarely offered on brief or single-visit consultations. Frequently, a consultant will hear a tentative plan and make suggestions for changes. One of the considerations in choosing the consultant may be how well those initial suggestions fit for you. As you would with any other professional you hire, ask colleagues and friends about potential consultants, interview several before choosing one, and get references which you do follow up on.

5. List Development Companies

A direct approach to getting lists of expansion phase M.C.O.s is through utilizing a list development company. In direct marketing, list development companies are frequently used, but they tend to be less often utilized in professional contract marketing. List development companies either find a list for a client or develop a list themselves; in either case, they charge on a per-name basis. Lists are usually developed from customer contacts or periodical subscriber information, but they can be compiled by direct telephone research. As a therapist, you are often the recipient of direct mail advertisements for continuing education sent from lists compiled from state licensure information or professional organizations. Formulating a list of expansion-phase behavioral managed care companies or a list of provider relations representatives who work for such M.C.O.s may be costly because it may be necessary to research the data for your one request. However, list development is a marketing tool that is sometimes undertaken by hospitals or hospital chains, so you might check with the marketing department of a local hospital to see if you can tap into their list before starting such an effort from scratch.

6. Marketing Companies

Sometimes, health provider marketing companies can be another resource for finding expansion-phase managed care companies in the local area. Marketing companies' primary function consists of helping their clients present themselves well, not finding contracting phase managed care organizations. But there is one service that a few marketing companies have begun to provide that can be quite valuable: acting as agents on the therapist's behalf. Because of the fast-changing nature of managed care and the convoluted proliferation of managed care products, many opportunities are emerging for provider responses. These can include getting on preferred provider panels or exclusive provider panels, joining other therapists to contract directly with a corporation for the mental health care of their employees, or making other arrangements. A few health care marketing companies are beginning to act like Hollywood agents — putting together deals so that various therapists they represent are packaged together and presented to a purchaser of the therapy services. If you can find a marketing firm doing this at an acceptable cost, you will be on the cutting edge of opportunities for therapists in the entire mental health care delivery market-place—including managed care.

7. Networking

One of the best ways to find expansion-phase M.C.O.s is through information obtained from personal contacts at meetings and conferences. There are three levels of meetings and two different groups that can be helpful for marketing to managed care companies: local and regional meetings, which are primarily held by the Employee Assistance Professionals' Association (E.A.P.A.), and national conferences, which are held by E.A.P.A. and by many managed care-related organizations.

Local Meetings

The most important local meetings are with employee assistance professionals. Throughout the United States (and in other countries), there are local chapters of the Employee Assistance Professionals Association. These chapters may range on a geographic basis from one that encompasses a part of a city all the way to some chapters that encompass half of a state. The E.A.P.A. chapter meetings can be particularly valuable because they can help the psychotherapist to understand the business context within which E.A.P.s make therapy referrals. Through these meetings, the therapist can acquaint himself with the vertical structure of the psychotherapy business as it applies to corporations and their referrals. They can also aid the therapist in recognizing who the influential people are in the local area, including those who make decisions about which therapists to use. (In managed care and business terms, these people are often referred to as "gate-keepers.")

As noted earlier, employee assistance providers are often quite influential with managed care companies in general. And they are usually especially knowledgeable about the managed care picture and marketplace in the local area. Since many managed care personnel come from the E.A.P. field and sometimes also return to that field, local chapter E.A.P. meetings can be quite helpful in getting to know whom to meet and in setting up those meetings.

Information about the location and time of local E.A.P. chapter meetings can be obtained through the chapter coordinator of the:

Employee Assistance Professionals Association, Inc.
4601 Fairfax Drive, Suite 10101
Arlington, Va. 22203

The telephone number for E.A.P.A.'s national office is (703) 522-6272. Other opportunities to meet E.A.P. and some managed care personnel occur at regional and national conferences of the Employee Assistance Professional Association and the reader may wish to inquire about these as well.

National Conferences

Although a regional and local chapter network is not available for meetings of managed care representatives per se, there are several national conferences at which it is usually possible to meet M.C.O. personnel. These meetings can be particularly fruitful in discovering which M.C.O.s will be expanding to your area. They can also provide an opportunity for meeting some of the provider relations personnel who will be choosing which therapist providers will be utilized by the managed care company. The following is a list of organizations that sponsored national or large regional managed care conferences in the past. Most of them can be expected to do follow-up conferences in the future:

Institute for International Research
Managed Behavioral Healthcare Conference
Conference Administrator, IIR
708 Third Avenue, 4th Floor
New York, N.Y. 10017-4103
(800) 345-8016

Infoline Inc.
Conference on The Changing Economic, Clinical & Market
    Realities of Managed Behavioral Healthcare
225 Turnpike Road
Southborough, Mass. 01772-1749
(508) 481-6400

P.I.S.L. Consulting Group
Workshop on Making Psychiatric Managed Care Work
7800 S. Elati #300
Littleton, Colo. 80120
(303) 794-1164

American Managed Care and Review Association
Annual Managed Care Conference & Exhibition
1227 25th Street, N.W., Suite 610
Washington, D.C. 20037

National Managed Health Care Congress
N.M.H.C.C.
Bay Colony Corporate Center
1000 Winter Street, Suite 4000
Waltham, Mass. 02154
(617) 487-6700

The National Managed Health Care Congress began offering a separate behavioral health care track in 1991. It is very large and provides an opportunity to get a feel for how behavioral health care fits into the larger managed care field along with medical health care.

Behavioral Healthcare Tomorrow
Institute for Behavioral Healthcare
Behavioral Healthcare Tomorrow Conference
4370 Alpine Road, Suite 108
Portola Valley, Calif. 94028
(415) 851-8411

The Behavioral Healthcare Tomorrow conference is especially recommended. It is large and usually sold out. This conference has taken place during the month of September for several years.

Behavioral managed care conferences are often more expensive than therapists are used to. Most of them are held primarily for the benefit of business people connected with managed care, so they tend to be scheduled during the business week (rather than the weekends, when most therapists' conferences are held). But because they cater primarily to the business people connected with managed care, they are potentially quite valuable for psychotherapists who wish to make contacts in this area. Also, your presence can be helpful to the business people and to the field in general. Probably, the best way to understand behavioral managed care is to see it as a vertically integrated system, with the therapists as the end providers of care. Since it is the therapists' services that are being marketed by all behavioral managed care companies, psychotherapist input can be very helpful at the conferences.

Should the reader wish to attend a behavioral managed care conference, it would probably be useful to get on the mailing list of several of the conference coordinators noted above. It can also be useful to speak with someone in the coordinator's office to ask:

1. Who usually attends the conference?
    The conference could cater to benefit managers, M.C.O. executives, provider relations personnel, case managers, utilization review managers, or psychotherapists. Generally, the more professions represented, the better. Of course, if it appeals to provider relations personnel, it will be particularly helpful for contacts because provider relations personnel are usually the people who are given the responsibility for deciding which therapists will be offered preferred provider contracts.
2. What is the usual size of the conference?
    Generally the larger the attendance the more opportunities you will have for personal contacts and the more discriminating you can be about the contacts.
3. Will there be formal networking opportunities or a display hall?
    When conference coordinators include formal networking opportunities, they demonstrate a recognition of the value of networking and a commitment to promote networking. A display hall nearly always promotes networking by its very nature.

Several suggestions are in order regarding personal contacts. Managed care personnel are usually extremely busy, so a brief introduction with a suggestion for later contact is a good policy. If the social situation allows for slightly longer contact, it is sometimes helpful to say a few things about your expertise or market niche. However, try to keep that to a minimum unless you get a clear indication from your contact that he or she wants to go further. Managed care people often really prefer to talk about generalities or personal points of interest when they are attending general conferences or E.A.P. chapter meetings. Generalized small talk can be useful. Often, you may find that it is more valuable to consider the initial contact to be an introduction, and to ask for the managed care person's business card plus permission to send information about oneself.

If this initial contact results in another meeting, the therapist can assume that the follow-up meeting will be business oriented. Prior to this meeting, the therapist should try to obtain as much information as possible about managed care in general and about the managed care company of the representative he or she will be meeting. M.C.O. personnel do not have time to educate therapists regarding managed care in general or even necessarily about their own managed care companies. Frequently, there are a large number of other therapists who are already familiar with the industry, and of course managed care personnel find it easiest to work with knowledge-able therapists.

By their very nature, insurance companies tend to be conservative, and managed care companies are often subsidiaries of insurance companies. Therefore, the managed care industry tends to be conservative. On the other hand, psychotherapists tend to be less conservative in dress and outlook. In addition, therapists and managed care business people tend to utilize different vocabularies. The therapist who wishes to make a good business impression with managed care companies should consider conservative dress in the form of a business suit for men and business attire for women, as well as a business vocabulary. It can be useful, therefore, to study the business terminology utilized by managed care. (Please see the glossary at the end of this book.) Also, it can be useful to read a copy of the *Wall Street Journal* or the business section of the local newspaper to orient oneself to business thinking just before a meeting with an M.C.O. business person.

One of the most successful therapists in dealing with managed care is Maurie Cullen, who is known by managed care personnel throughout the country and appears as both a presenter and panelist for some of the most prestigious conferences on managed care. The secret of her success is her ability at networking. She provides below several insights into the elements of successful networking for marketing in a managed care environment:

1. "We (therapists) are in a person-to-person business, and there is no magic or formula to approaching people. It is important to show interest, kindness, and to present oneself as a helpful resource."[4] "In approaching any managed care organization staff people, we need to ask, 'What can I do to help you?' rather than present our own needs in an assertive manner.

2. "As providers we need to take a diplomatic approach in our marketing strategies. It is productive to view our colleagues in managed care as we view ourselves and think about how we would want to be approached. If we think about that initially before going into the networking, we are at an advantage.

3. "Don't assume that people are comfortable and confident. Help them become comfortable and confident with your own congeniality.

4. "As providers, we are seeking to build a reputation of consistency and stability. So we need to demonstrate that in relationships with managed care colleagues.

5. "We need to work with the system of managed care, not against it. And we need to find a way to fit in. If there is a change that we see to be necessary for effectiveness, we can become productive voices for that change.
6. "If we do run up against difficulties with managed care, we need to take a positively proactive—but not angry—position."[5]

HOW NOT TO DO IT

A worst-case example of how to not do marketing might help. Mr. Naive is a therapist who had maintained a successful practice for two years prior to the advent of managed care. Suddenly, his practice began to disappear as many of the clients who had previously seen him were now covered by managed care—and he was on no managed care provider lists. He found that a major managed care conference was to be held in his town. Mr. Naive attended the conference and came prepared in that he brought along a number of business cards and publicity materials about the groups he was doing. Upon entering the conference area of the hotel, Mr. Naive discovered that everyone was dressed in suits. Although he had thought to wear a jacket, he wore jeans and had no tie; he found it difficult to fit in. He did not think about his earring, but he considered that a part of his personality and therefore irrelevant from his perspective.

Mr. Naive saw several people conversing and approached them, saying: "Is this the A.B.C. managed care conference?"

One of the men answered, "Yes."

"Cool. I need to meet some of you folks, so I can get patients from you."

The man responded, "Well, we are benefit managers. We don't make referrals."

Mr. Naive said, "Benny what?" But the men had returned to their conversation and were studiously ignoring him. Not to be deterred, however, Mr. Naive saw another man alone and approached him, asking, "Are you a benny something or do you refer clients to therapists?"

While looking for a place to hide, the man answered, "I work with someone who refers clients, but our provider list is full."

Mr. Naive grew enthusiastic. Pulling out his P.R. material and a business card, he said, "Please tell your friend about me. I have been in practice two years and I'm excellent at everything; postpartum depression, senility, schizophrenia, multiple personalities. But I'm really good at past life regressions and working with teenagers." (He genuinely was skilled in working with adolescents.)

The man took his card and said, "I'll see what I can do."

The rest of the day continued in a similar manner. Although he got little encouragement, Mr. Naive went home happy with his endeavor. The only problem was that six months later he still had no managed care referrals — or any prospects of getting them.

Ultimately, Mr. Naive spoke to a colleague about marketing. He changed his approach along the lines we have discussed, utilizing niche marketing for a specialization with adolescents. He subscribed to a couple of journals and newsletters and became familiar with who was contracting in his area. When he attended another conference, he enrolled and looked at who would be attending so that he could plan out whom he wanted to contact. The contacts were brief, respectful, to the point, and couched in business terminology. Although Mr. Naive began to wear a suit, he kept his earring and turned it to his advantage, using it as an attention-getter. If a businessperson acknowledged his earring, Mr. Naive pointed out how he uses it to help adolescents feel comfortable more quickly when they are working with him. And eventually he began to receive referrals from managed care companies for adolescent work.

SUMMARY

In this chapter we have discussed contracting cycles and the importance of timing in marketing to managed care companies. We have looked at methods to find expansion-phase M.C.O.s including use of therapists' national professional organizations, publications, list development companies, behavioral health hospitals, managed care consultants, health care marketing companies, and meetings and conferences. Finally, we have considered how to approach personal contracts and how not to. But even with all of these efforts to find expansion-phase M.C.O.s, you will miss some. And you will probably reach a number of managed care companies after their preferred provider panels are full. As life sometimes has it, those may be some of the very M.C.O.s you most want to affiliate with. If that is the case, please read on, because breaking into "closed" panels is what the next chapter is about.

NOTES

1. This information was obtained in a telephone interview between Ruth Yoshpe, M.D. and the author on 11-18-92.
2. This information was obtained in a telephone interview between Lizbet Boroughs and the author on 11-18-92, and amended on 6-07-93.
3. Private verbal communication on 3-4-93 by Maurie Cullen, M.S.W., B.C.D.
4. From private interview with Maurie Cullen, M.S.W., B.C.D. on 4-6-94.
5. From private interview with Maurie Cullen, M.S.W., B.C.D. on 4-6-93.

3/
Breaking into Closed Provider Lists

As was noted in the previous chapter, clinicians frequently find out about a managed care organization only after that M.C.O. has concluded its contract with a local major employer. And that is almost always too late for the therapist to apply for provider status with the M.C.O, since there are no longer any **official** openings for new providers.

When therapists hear that the preferred provider list is closed, they often either become angry or just give up. Both are understandable reactions, but a more pragmatic approach is recommended. It is especially valuable to realize that when a managed care preferred provider panel is pronounced closed, it is rarely totally closed! Dr. Michael Glasser, the western regional medical director for American PsychManagement, Inc., has noted, "We say the door is closed, but not locked."[1] Therefore, any opportunity to market your practice to a "closed" M.C.O. you are interested in joining should be utilized. That is particularly true when you have contact with staff members of a managed care company.

In the last few years, a painful scenario has begun to occur with increasing frequency across the country. A therapist and a patient have begun to work well together, but the patient's employer changes its behavioral health benefits. The new benefit structure automatically enrolls the patient into a managed care company. At that point, the patient is given one of two choices: (1) to go to a therapist who is on the M.C.O.'s list of preferred providers and receive substantial help from the insurance company in paying the bill or (2) to go to an out-of-network therapist and receive little or no help from the insurance company in paying the bill. Having never heard of that M.C.O. before, the present therapist is out-of-network (i.e., not on the provider list of the managed care company).

The therapist states that he is willing to become a preferred provider and contacts the managed care company, requesting an application for that purpose. The therapist is told that the M.C.O. no longer has openings for new providers. Thus, the patient and therapist are faced with the choice of terminating their relationship so that the patient can transfer to an in-network therapist or working together under a financial arrangement in which the patient must pay most or all of the therapy bill, even though the patient's employer is purchasing behavioral health insurance benefits on his or her behalf.

When this occurs, there are several things the therapist can do. One of the first inclinations of the therapist will be to bring up the issue of continuity of care with the provider relations staff. It is helpful to gently inquire about the M.C.O.'s policy regarding continuity of care because often the M.C.O. has made at least a token effort to address this. When continuity of care is addressed, it usually is in the form of the M.C.O. agreeing to a three-to-six-month grace period during which the patient can either terminate therapy altogether or close off with the present therapist in preparation for a transfer to a future in-network therapist.

Sometimes, there is no provision for a grace period or the therapist will conclude that the M.C.O. has not addressed the question of continuity of care sufficiently. At that point, the clinician will probably be tempted to make a more forceful argument in favor of continuity of care. Unless this is done very carefully, it is probably not in the best interest of either the therapist or the patient. The patient may well be angry about lack of continuity of care and will probably need careful help from the therapist to work through this. But a heated discussion between therapist and managed care representative carries a substantial chance of spilling over onto the patient from either the therapist or the M.C.O. staff.

In most cases, the M.C.O. representative will be someone on the provider relations staff. Generally (but not always), M.C.O.s staff their provider relations departments with licensed clinicians. Those clinicians are already very aware of continuity of care issues. In most M.C.O.s with poor continuity of care policies, the provider relations clinicians are constantly pushing to upgrade those policies — and probably the legal departments are also pushing for policy upgrades in this area. If the therapist can make constructive suggestions to further this effort, the therapist will be seen as a hero. However, if he or she only criticizes, the therapist will probably be seen as a pest — and a pest who has reminded the provider relations staff of their own powerlessness! This is poor relationship building — and poor marketing.

On the other hand, if there is a grace period, it offers two potential marketing opportunities to the therapist in his or her effort to break into this closed provider list. Public relations specialists say that in order for a product to be recognized and remembered by a potential consumer, it needs to be seen between six and 12 times. It can be useful for the therapist to consider himself as a product in this regard. The continuity of care grace period can be seen as an opportunity to begin those contacts. And the contacts can be with both provider relations representatives and case managers.

Provider relations representatives are the people who make most of the decisions about who will be included as a preferred provider, so contacts with them are the most important. If the clinician is able to favorably impress the provider relations representative over a number of contacts, the representative will have an incentive to think of that therapist when openings occur at a later date in the therapist's local geographic area. The favorable impression can be fostered through a demonstration of:

1. sophistication with managed care perspectives (which can be obtained through reading this book),
2. capability in particular skills and training that are especially valued by M.C.O.s (see Chapter 5), and
3. sensitivity to (not necessarily agreement with) managed care policies and issues.

While personal contacts with provider relations personnel are useful when one is seeking to break into a "closed" managed care provider panel, they can also be useful for future contracting. Frequently, when a managed care company expands to a new area, it hires provider relations representatives who are experienced with previously established M.C.O.s in that area. And those representatives bring their personal contacts along to the new M.C.O. This means that the therapist who has connected well with such a provider relations representative will probably find it easier to become a part of the provider network for the expanding M.C.O.

Contacts with case managers can also be useful. Case managers are the managed care personnel who, in fact, manage the care. They ask therapists for reports outlining the rationale for and progress of treatment. And all treatment requires authorization from the case managers before payment will be made. Case managers are nearly always licensed clinicians who are usually assigned on a local geographic basis, even when the M.C.O. staff is headquartered thousands of miles away. For example, the M.C.O. staff may be in Dallas but a particular case manager will be assigned to work only with patients and providers in the western San Fernando Valley section of Los Angeles.

In this way, the case manager will get to know the approved therapists in that specific region. The case manager will begin to get an understanding regarding which therapists genuinely have special expertise in specific specialty areas and which therapists just say they do. And he or she will begin to find out where holes in areas of expertise exist, and will also quickly discover which therapists are easy to work with and which are not. If the non-network therapist (who has contact with the case manager only around a patient who is in the grace period) impresses the case manager, that contact can sometimes break open a place on the preferred provider list. Sometimes, after an M.C.O. has begun to service an account for awhile and holes in the network begin to become apparent, it is possible for the case manager to go to the provider relations department and request inclusion into the network of a particular therapist who he or she feels would be particularly suited to fill that hole.

GROUP CONTRACTING TO BREAK INTO "CLOSED" M.C.O.s

Probably the most effective way to break into officially closed provider panels is through group contracting. During the past year, a strong movement has gained momentum among major M.C.O.s to encourage contracting with groups of psychotherapist providers. M.C.O.s experience many advantages in contracting with provider groups. It allows the managed care company to negotiate fee arrangements. This contrasts with the structural necessity of maintaining a set fee system for individual provider contracts. Negotiated fee arrangements allow the M.C.O. to shift part or all of the financial risk to the provider groups. (See Chapter 7 for a full explanation of this.) Just as importantly, group contracting allows the managed care company to shift responsibility to the provider group for all special reports, quality assurance, and utilization review.

All of these advantages to the managed care companies carry corresponding potential disadvantages to therapists who contract on a group basis, so you should be very careful about this kind of contracting. We will discuss more about the advantages and disadvantages of group contracting in Chapter 7. Nevertheless, if the structure of the contract is an acceptable one, group contracting can be an extremely effective way to break into closed provider lists. Dr. Glasser (see above) has stated, "Managed care companies are always interested in multidiscipline groups who have developed quality, cost-effective outpatient treatment. Additionally, groups that are able to do their own U.R./Q.A. (See Chapter 7) will have an edge in the managed care arena. Outcomes will determine who gets the work and who doesn't."[2]

NICHE MARKETING TO BREAK INTO "CLOSED" M.C.O.s

Another way to break into officially closed provider panels is to offer the M.C.O. something special it needs. You can usually make this breakthrough by providing a skill, specialization, or location that is lacking in the provider mix that the M.C.O. presently has available to offer its subscribers.

The skill most frequently needed is the ability to conduct therapy in a foreign language or in sign language. Although facility in a foreign language is not a skill that is easily acquired, if the therapist already has this skill it should be exploited. One language that some feel is relatively easily learned is sign language. And sign language is frequently needed by managed care companies. Should the reader wish to develop a skill in sign language, it could well open some doors. But before undertaking such an effort, the best policy would be to check first with the managed care companies the reader wishes to join to ensure that this effort would pay off in acceptance on the preferred provider panel.

If you are a member of an ethnic or sexual minority, you should definitely emphasize that status. Patients from these groups are often concerned about potential bias on the part of therapists, even if it is unintentional. (Some Latinos and African-Americans are very aware of the cultural biases that predispose the results of frequently utilized tests against them. Middle-age and older gay men and lesbians often remember when their sexual orientation itself was considered an illness.) Therefore some are insistent upon obtaining a therapist who comes from the same minority.

A related area that can be considered a specialty is familiarity with a subculture or subgroup (such as Armenians, holocaust survivors, disabled people, born-again Christians, to name only a few). Even without foreign language skills, specialized knowledge of a subculture or subgroup can be particularly helpful to marketing because patients in those groups frequently request therapists who are familiar with their culture or subgroup. In some cases, such as among some born-again Christians, clients may even feel that they will be endangered unless the therapist is sympathetic with their beliefs. Sophisticated M.C.O.s try to respond to these requests since client satisfaction is a major factor in determining whether or not corporations choose to renew contracts with the M.C.O.

Other specialty areas can be equally helpful. For example, gambling addiction and fear of flying are sufficiently uncommon that they may not already be covered by clinicians enrolled with some M.C.O.s.

Some M.C.O.s are not aware of the need to offer less frequently requested specialties or they prefer to not extend the extra effort or expense of providing for these. But value-based M.C.O.s (see Chapter 6) are very aware of the need to offer particular specialties, and they engage in a proactive effort to fill those gaps in their network. Often, M.C.O.s will utilize their provider newsletter to alert therapists to a particular specialization need. Therefore, it can be quite useful to read such newsletters. If a therapist is interested in contracting with a particular managed care organization and is locked out, he or she should always ask to at least be placed on the mailing list for the provider newsletter or arrange with a colleague to regularly review his or her copy.

Location can be an especially valuable tool for opening opportunities in an otherwise closed managed care organization. As noted previously, contracts between M.C.O.s and the corporations that purchase their services usually require therapist provider coverage that is geographically dispersed sufficiently to offer convenient services to every employee, dependent, and retiree. Most M.C.O.s experience some difficulty in meeting this requirement. It is often especially difficult to provide therapist coverage in resort areas, since those areas tend to be populated primarily by transient vacationers and by retirees.

While it is usually unrealistic for a therapist to consider moving in order to get included in a managed care organization, sometimes a partial office relocation is possible with little effort. If the therapist has a second home in a resort area where he or she usually spends weekends, it might be worthwhile to consider spending Friday through Sunday or Saturday through Monday at the second home and open a one-day-a-week office in the resort area on Fridays or Mondays. So far, most M.C.O.s that have included a therapist on their preferred provider list because of the location of a second office have included the primary office location as well.

Should the reader wish to do this, the same caveat applies as mentioned earlier regarding learning sign language. Opening a second office primarily for the purpose of getting into a managed care organization should be preceded by an inquiry to the M.C.O. as to whether or not it would agree to add the therapist to its list of preferred providers should such a second office be opened. The M.C.O.'s policy regarding primary office inclusion should also be clarified.

PERSONAL CONTACTS

Personal contacts are another effective way of breaking into a "closed" managed care company. One way of extending such contacts is through developing and offering needed special training for therapists. Increasing numbers of provider relations departments are seeking to extend their preferred providers' expertise in such areas as levels of treatment (to maximize appropriate treatment, reduce in-patient hospitalization, etc.) and brief therapy. If the therapist has an expertise in a needed area and is willing to provide such training, the training process can constitute an opportunity to meet with provider relations staffs.

A number of corporations have found it valuable to retain their own employee assistance professionals (E.A.P.s) when they sign with managed care organizations, even though some of the traditional E.A.P. functions can be subsumed under the managed care contract. When this happens, the E.A.P. has continuous contact with the M.C.O. and frequently is in a position to suggest inclusion of a particular therapist as a preferred provider. The E.A.P. is likely to make such a recommendation if the therapist is seen as having an especially useful expertise or if a number of employees are asking for the particular therapist.

Because of their multiple possible functions within corporations, there are often a number of ways to meet employee assistance providers. Referring to the new functions corporations are asking E.A.P.s to fulfill and to the old functions sometimes being undertaken by M.C.O.s, Dr. Bradley Googins has noted that the very identification of what constitutes an E.A.P. is getting reshaped at the moment.[3] Six of the functions that can be a part of an E.A.P.'s responsibilities carry special opportunities for therapists who wish to meet E.A.P.s. They are:

1. Corporate crisis response programs such as critical incidence debriefings,
2. wellness or prevention programs,
3. downsizing support programs,
4. financial counselling,
5. risk management for stress-related worker's compensation, and
6. work-family coordination (including child care and elder care).

If the therapist keeps alert to business developments in his local geographical area, he can be aware of contact opportunities resulting from business crises. After a bank holdup, there is a need for crisis intervention and critical incident debriefings. When large layoffs or cutbacks occur, there is a need for outplacement emotional transition planning. These and some other services — such as worker's compensation risk management and some forms of financial counselling (not financial planning) — are often contracted out on a consultant basis rather than assigned to behavioral health providers through the preferred provider network. The therapist who is — or can become — skilled in these areas may open up a "back door" entry to contracting directly with an influential employee assistance professional. Of course, you can further interest the E.A.P. if you offer the services on a pro bono or reduced cost basis the first time as a way of introducing yourself.

One of the corporate functions that often gets assigned to E.A.P.s is responsibility for a wellness program. Usually, additional funding or staffing is not made available to the E.A.P. to cover this wellness function. Therefore, E.A.P.s often turn to therapists in their community, requesting that the therapist speak at a "brown bag lunch" for employees as a means of meeting the employee assistance program's wellness responsibilities. (The therapist is often asked to do a pro bono presentation, usually at lunch time.) The talk is on a wellness topic.

When a therapist is asked to do a "brown bag" lunch presentation for an E.A.P. of a corporation that has a managed care contract with an M.C.O. which the therapist is locked out of, two opportunities become available for breaking into the M.C.O. The therapist must coordinate with the E.A.P. regarding delivery of the speech and the E.A.P. usually sits in on the speech. If these contacts result in the E.A.P. becoming impressed with the therapist, he or she will have an incentive to push for inclusion of the therapist on the M.C.O.'s preferred provider list. Additionally, the speech itself may result in a number of employees wanting to obtain counselling from the therapist, thus creating a client-driven need.

Although the nature of most M.C.O.-corporation contracts makes it difficult for M.C.O.s to be totally responsive to all client requests, a whole group of requests would probably result in much more serious consideration on the part of the preferred provider staff. This is particularly true if the requests happen to come at a time close to the renewal date of the M.C.O.-corporation's contract. Such timing is usually a matter of luck. But if the therapist is asked to make a speech and finds out that the anticipated date of the speech will be after the corporate-M.C.O. contract renewal date, he or she should definitely ask if the speech could be given at an earlier date.

Breaking into a managed care company through direct contact with an E.A.P. is usually somewhat involved, because of the complicated relationship E.A.P.s often have with managed care companies. An understanding of this relationship is imperative if the therapist wishes to market to E.A.P.s in order to break into "closed" managed care companies.

In some corporations the initiative to contract with a managed care company comes from the employee assistance program department. When that occurs, the E.A.P. is usually very influential in deciding which M.C.O. to use. And the M.C.O. personnel usually understand that they must work closely and cooperatively with the E.A.P. in order to make the contract work and in order to get a contract renewal at the end of the initial contract period. In other cases, the initial decision to investigate contracting with a managed care company comes from the corporate benefits department. In the most abrasive situations, this decision arises primarily out of a desire to reduce benefits costs and the E.A.P. has been seen as a financial drain which must be controlled. (E.A.P.s can cite studies demonstrating cost savings over the long term, but benefit managers are often judged on their short-term performance and therefore see long-term cost savings as considerably less relevant.) Usually the situation consists of something between these two extremes.

The important point for therapists to know is that E.A.P.s have potential influence upon the selection of providers, but that influence generally needs to be wielded carefully. So if an E.A.P. is impressed by a therapist and wants that therapist on the preferred list, the E.A.P. may still wait for a politically opportune moment before acting on the recommendation. This can mean a delay of up to a year before the therapist begins seeing referrals from the M.C.O. Patience is a necessity.

If you wish to consider working with E.A.P.s for the purpose of breaking into a particular M.C.O., you will probably wish to target those E.A.P.s associated with companies who contract with the particular M.C.O. The easiest way to find these companies is to ask the M.C.O. for a list of companies they contract with. Some M.C.O.s will be unwilling to provide such a list. When that happens, it is another reason to get on the mailing list of the M.C.O.'s provider newsletter, which often announces new contracts and refers to existing contracts.

THE INTEREST LETTER

Whether or not one has a recommendation from an E.A.P. or other insider, it can be useful to request an application initially by mail. This makes it possible to use a verbal follow-up later. The request for an application (i.e., the interest letter) should be short and to the point. At the same time, it can be useful to include information in the letter that may lead a marginal M.C.O. to open its list to you. This is especially desirable if the M.C.O. has most of its providers in place but still has a need for specialized providers. The best way to do a short letter that still emphasizes your strengths is to make it in "bullet" form. Attached, (Figure 3) you will find a sample of a bullet interest letter.

SUMMARY

Breaking into closed provider lists is one of the most difficult tasks confronting a therapist who wishes to contract with M.C.O.s. In this chapter we have examined a number of ways to accomplish that task, including utilizing the continuity of care grace period, favorable name recognition with provider relations staff and case managers, group contracting, niche marketing, office location or relocation, and personal contacts. Once you have extended all of this effort and received a contract, you may feel that the hard part of marketing is over. But there are two additional primary marketing challenges to complete before a sustained flow of referrals from M.C.O.s will result: referral development and retention on the most-actively-referred-to-providers list. In the next chapter we will discuss referral development.

Date

John Jones, L.C.S.W.
XYZH Corp.
1234 Alphabet Street
Anywhere, Tex. 11111

Dear Mr. Jones:

In the December 25, 1999 issue of "Behavioral Healthcare Benefits Journal" an article mentioned that XYZH Corporation will be expanding to the Pascagula area of North Texas. I am interested in becoming a provider for XYZH Corporation, and I believe that the following items should make me an attractive addition to your provider mix in the North Texas area:

- 49 years of private practice in Pascagula,

- Brief therapy expertise as demonstrated by several journal publications,

- Certified expertise in somatoform pain disorder,

- Up to three years of experience with over 10 managed care companies as a preferred provider,

- Up to two years of experience with three managed care companies as an E.A.P. provider,

- Multicultural training and Sensitivity by training to visually-impaired clients.

I hope you agree that I would make a good preferred provider for XYZH's network in Pascagula. I will be contacting you in the next couple of weeks to discuss this further. In the meantime, if you would like any additional information, please feel free to contact me at the above telephone number and address.

Sincerely,

Janet Businessperson, L.C.S.W.

Figure 3: Example of Bullet Interest Letter

NOTES

1. This was emphasized in a speech "Treatment Modalities and Levels of Care from a Managed Care Perspective" delivered by Michael Glasser, M.D. at Charter Thousand Oaks Hospital on 11/19/92.
2. Ibid.
3. Bradley Googins, Ph.D., Professor at Boston University School of Social Work, Boston, Ma. Quote is from his participation on a panel "To Be or Not To Be" on 11-01-92 at the 21st annual conference of the Employee Assistance Professional Association, Inc.

4/
The Second Marketing Challenge: Referral Development

There is one primary rationale that M.C.O.s have used to justify asking preferred providers to lower their fees for clients referred through the M.C.O. It is that providers will save P.R. costs since the M.C.O. will provide a stream of referrals to the therapists. Sometimes that occurs, but it is rarely automatic. In most cases, therapists need to exert a substantial referral development effort after they are accepted on the preferred provider network.

In this chapter, we will consider several aspects of this second challenge of marketing to the managed care companies. The best, easiest, and first marketing tool for referral development consists of your preferred provider application, so most of this chapter will concern itself with the application. Even though Chapter 5 primarily addresses the issue of how to stay on the active provider list, it carries substantial material that is applicable to initial referral development as well. You will find that your ongoing contacts with the M.C.O. will be monitored and compiled into a provider profile. And the provider profile will usually have a strong impact upon additional referrals. This means that the quality of your work and your reports will influence how frequently referrals are made to you.

Finally, your contact with your case manager and others in the M.C.O. will substantially enhance or hinder your chances of obtaining additional referrals. Thus, the material discussed in Chapters 4 and 5 should be taken together as forming a continuum of issues affecting referral development, and they reflect the fact that marketing is a continuous process.

THE APPLICATION: YOUR *BEST* MARKETING TOOL

When you receive an application from a managed care company, you can usually breath a sigh of relief and know that your first marketing challenge is essentially conquered. It is rare for an M.C.O. to send an application to a therapist unless it is fairly sure of wanting that therapist on its network of preferred providers. The various costs of sending applications is too high to send them without intending to contract. Since contracting is a fairly sure thing regardless of when or how well you complete the application, you may be tempted to delay completing it or to complete it in the most expedient manner.

Don't!

Please take the opposite position. Try to complete the application quickly and very, very carefully.

You should consider the application as the one best chance you will have to communicate directly with those who make decisions about referrals—for the duration of the time you are on that panel of preferred providers. To understand this, let's review how referrals are usually handled. In most M.C.O.s, when a client has a problem he or she calls a central 800 number and is connected with an intake person who is skilled at assessment, triage, and referral. If the intake person feels the client is appropriate for an outpatient referral, he or she uses the computer to call up a list of therapists in the client's local area, then screens for specialty unless there are specific factors such as the need for handicapped access or cultural identification, or client preference regarding a certain kind of therapist. It is this two-step, computer-aided search that determines the therapist for most referrals. And the raw material that goes into the computer comes primarily from provider applications. The most important part of the application is the part that asks about your specialties.

SPECIALTIES

Look for the section in the application marked "Specialties." For legal reasons, it may be labeled "Areas of Interest" or some similar title. In most cases, a list of specialties will be presented with check-off boxes. The application instructions will request that you check off those specialties in which you claim expertise. You will be asked to check no more than 1/2 to 2/3 of the specialties listed. If you are like most therapists who have been in private practice for some time, you will have probably developed some experience in many different areas, so that there is a good chance you will have to make some choices.

Expertise Validation Packet

Of course, the first determinant of the specialties you claim expertise in should be, "What are the fields in which you hold a combination of experience, training, and interest?" Use this criterion for all of the specializations you claim.

In their application packets, many managed care companies ask for verification of the training that supports your claims of expertise. You will find that it generally pays off if you provide extensive information about this, listing your expertise in easily assimilated form. One way to accomplish that is to include a separate packet with your application for this purpose. The packet can begin with one sheet providing an overview of your specialties and the page numbers of attached sheets where they are listed. Then take a separate page for each specialty and include:

1. Certifications
2. Dates and locations of any teaching you have done on the subject with most recent dates first,
3. Any articles or books you have written on the subject,
4. Experience,
5. Training you have attended on the subject (listing titles of workshops or seminars in date order, starting with the most recent first),
6. Articles or books you have read and utilize extensively.

I suggest that you assemble this expertise validation packet once, make multiple copies, and send it out with each application. When the application asks for expertise validation, you can simply write in "See Attached Expertise Validation Packet." Be sure to continue updating your packet since managed care organizations are usually especially interested in your most recent training.

An expertise validation packet is a fair amount of work, and you may wonder if it is necessary. There are probably some M.C.O.s that will not care. But in Chapter 6 we will be discussing the desirability of your trying to affiliate primarily with M.C.O.s that are particularly concerned with quality; those M.C.O.s will care a great deal about this validation. It is rare to get feedback from managed care companies about applications. The author has received positive feedback from two clinical directors about the expertise validation packet he has sent. Since most of the work of compiling such a packet is a one-time effort, you will probably find it worthwhile.

Strategic Specialty Choices

If the breadth of your training and experience provide you with more areas of expertise than the application allows you to check off, you should consider making strategic choices.

Begin by getting in the running for most-frequently-referred diagnoses.

I suggest that you begin by checking off (if appropriate) mood disorders, anxiety disorders, adjustment disorders, and marital counselling since these four probably account for about 65% of the diagnoses treated by the average M.C.O. One silver lining to managed care is that marriage counselling is often covered; it was not usually reimbursed by indemnity insurance since it is a V code in the DSM-IV. If the application lists marital problems as a choice, you can be pretty sure that marriage counselling is covered.

Once you have listed the above four specialties, please be aware that you have only kept yourself in the running for clients with those diagnoses. But you probably have not placed yourself in any competitively advantageous position, since most of the therapists in your geographic area will probably check the same specialties.

Distinguish yourself from colleagues.

Since the referral process in most M.C.O.s is a two-step process that compares you to all other preferred providers in your geographic area, it is important that you try to distinguish yourself from your local colleagues by indicating specialized expertise that other therapists don't usually have. The best way to accomplish this is to indicate any special abilities that are important to a particular group of potential patients. Three of these special populations are:

1. Non-English speaking patients.
   Any bilingual capability is helpful, but especially Spanish in Florida and the southwest and French in New England.
2. Geographic and ethnic minorities.
   This is especially appreciated if there are large minority communities in your geographic region. If you are part of a minority (Asian, Arabic, African-American, etc.), emphasize that fact strongly.
3. Cultural, sexual, and religious minorities.
   Gays, lesbians, born-again Christians, Jews, law enforcement officers, physically impaired people, and those in other minority groups and cultures with special needs appreciate therapists who understand and are sensitive to their needs.

If you are not part of a minority but are familiar with and sensitive to the issues of a minority, you do not need to let your lack of minority status stop you from claiming an expertise in this area. But you should indicate your non-minority status by checking a box and then writing "sensitive" after it (Example: Police-sensitive, Blind-sensitive, Cuban-sensitive). One of the problems some M.C.O.s have experienced is sending a patient to a therapist who is described by the intake person as part of a minority and the therapist turns out to not be. Although the therapist will probably do an excellent job with that client because he has sensitized himself to the special issues (or he would not have checked the box), a perceptual problem can occur that often complicates the treatment (and leaves the M.C.O. in a bad light with its client corporation) unless the therapist is described as minority sensitive instead of a part of a minority.

Managed care companies are aware of the fact that therapists who are part of minority cultures are knowledgeable about which of the usual rules of therapy to break in order to be effective. And quality-based managed care companies know that one of the services they are well-positioned to accentuate in their own marketing is a connection between the patient and the most appropriate local therapist. Many managed care companies provide this only on a lip-service basis. But as M.C.O.s begin to compete in the marketplace more on the basis of service (see Chapter 5), the effort to fit clients who have minority concerns with therapists who have expertise in minority issues will become increasingly meaningful. And this should result in a larger referral flow to you if you have indicated a minority status or a minority-sensitive expertise.

Underserved Specialties

After minority specialties, one of the most productive ways to distinguish yourself from other colleagues in your area is to emphasize any specialties that managed care companies experience as relatively underserved. Expertise in working with young children is the most frequently cited underserved specialty area, according to M.C.O. personnel I have spoken with. There are two other specialties M.C.O.s have indicated they frequently need but have experienced occasional difficulty in finding therapists for. They are pain management (certification usually required) and skill in dealing with workers' compensation cases.

Infrequently Offered Specializations

The next best way to distinguish yourself from colleagues in your area is to check off any infrequently offered areas of specialization. Two of these offered by colleagues of mine are stepfamily adjustment and T.M.J. Syndrome (Temporomandibular Joint Disorder, the most common symptom of which is grinding of the teeth). These have constituted the bedrock upon which each of these therapists has built a good practice.

Unlisted Specializations

Usually, infrequently offered specializations are not included in the listings that managed care companies make available for check-off on their specialization lists. However, a blank line will often be left where additional specialties can be written in. When that option is available, it can be an extremely valuable option under some circumstances and a genuine waste of one of your choices under other circumstances. The distinction between these is dependent upon whether or not this specialty makes it onto the M.C.O.'s computer. If there is a box next to the write-in line, it often indicates that the write-in has a space on the computer field. If there is no box or other indication that this choice will be computerized, you will be better off not utilizing the write-in option. When it is computerized, the write-in is one of the most valuable choices you can make because even though few patients will request this particular service, the probability is very high that you will get 100% of the referrals of the patients who do request or need it.

Special Needs

Most M.C.O.s offer an assessment and referral service option to corporations with which they contract. Many major corporations have employee assistance programs already in place and do not avail themselves of this, but smaller companies often do utilize this service. In order to offer the assessment and referral service, many M.C.O.s set up a separate group of clinicians to specifically evaluate and refer. Sometimes, this clinician group consists of full-time employees of the managed care company. But frequently, M.C.O.s fulfill this function through separate contracting with private practice providers. When an M.C.O. contracts for supplemental services from private practice clinicians for evaluation and referral, they often ask separate questions in their application regarding therapists' capabilities in this area. At other times, however, this panel gets contracted on a hit-or-miss basis. So if you carry an expertise in assessment and referral and you do not see another place on the application to highlight it, write it in under "Specialties." Since the assessment and referral function is either parallel to or supplemental to that of intake clinicians who utilize the computer to refer to specialties, a need for this expertise to show up on the computer is rarely relevant.

In an era of across the board corporate cost-cutting, many corporations ask their outside vendors (M.C.O.s) to help them with downsizing. Often, they will hire an outplacement agency to help employees find new jobs and a retirement planning firm to deal with early retirement issues. In addition, they frequently seek to complete the services picture by contracting with their previously-contracted M.C.O. to help with job-loss trauma and the emotional aspects of the change. Since most outplacement agencies are very expensive, M.C.O.s are sometimes asked to cover that function as well— especially for line workers. When this occurs, the managed care companies need to figure out which of their contracted providers holds expertise in this area. It is rare for an application to ask specifically about providers' capability for helping with job-loss trauma or career planning. If you have expertise in these areas, it can be helpful to write that in on the blank spaces under "Specialties."

Skills in critical incident debriefing are especially valuable to particular industries. For example, the banking industry is vulnerable to especially traumatic large-scale robberies. If you have expertise in critical incident debriefing, emphasize it. But keep in mind that any time you write a specialty into a blank space, you must clarify whether or not it will make it onto the computer (except for assessment and referral).

AIDS is increasingly impacting the workplace. If you have experience working with AIDS — particularly if you hold expertise in defusing potential workplace legal issues arising from AIDS — note that on your application.

In Chapters 5 and 7 we will be referring to substance abuse issues that reflect the need experienced by M.C.O.s for clinicians who have expertise in the substance abuse arena. Since substance abuse is a disease of denial, patients often do not come into treatment until very late in the disease process. Medical offset studies have increasingly alerted corporations to the costs of this delay. In recent years, a process for helping substance abusers "hit bottom" (accept the need for treatment) has been developed. It is called "intervention." If you are an experienced and trained interventionist, emphasize that in your application.

Specialties to Avoid

Just as there are some specialties that are good choices to make, there are also specialties that should not be chosen if you wish to maximize your referrals.

Except for the frequently requested diagnoses, it is probably better to stay away from overserved specialties such as sex abuse or post-traumatic stress. The larger the number of therapists who check off a given specialization, the less chance any given therapist has of receiving a referral for it.

Unless there is some contraindicating circumstance, you should also avoid DSM-IV Axis II diagnoses (developmental disorders and personality disorders). Managed care companies complete their contracts with corporations on a customized basis, usually including just about any provisions that fit for that corporation. To keep costs down, benefit managers frequently ask for coverage only for acute pathology, excluding any diagnosis that could be considered to be chronic. The resulting mix of contracts means that a significant percentage of clients who would be appropriate for an Axis II referral cannot be referred to you because they are not covered for that diagnosis.

Many problems can result from this if you indicate an expertise in Axis II disorders. One of them is that you will have a lower statistical probability of a referral resulting from indicating an Axis II disorder expertise than would result from most other choices. Another is that Axis II patients often have symptoms of other diagnoses as well. If a client is not covered under an Axis II diagnosis, he may be referred to you under a co-existing Axis I diagnosis instead, because the intake person saw that you have expertise in the Axis II area and geographically similar therapists with the same Axis I expertise do not. But the treatment authorizations for Axis I are, understandably, considerably less than those under Axis II in most cases. Therefore, you can end up with a patient who may need additional treatment but who is not covered for it. Unless the client can pay out-of-pocket, you may be stuck because of patient abandonment ethics.

Medical Necessity

A final group of diagnoses to avoid consists of those for which medical necessity is questionable. We have already discussed marital conflict. If it is listed as a check-off, it is probably covered. If it is not listed as a check-off, do not write it in, because it will almost certainly not be covered. Another commonly treated condition that usually does not qualify under medical necessity is codependency. The author does a great deal of work with sexual addiction. But I rarely use one of my check-offs to designate this as an area of expertise, since it is frequently not considered to be covered under medical necessity. However, I am seeking to acquaint M.C.O.s with the desirability of changing that omission. If there is any question in your mind regarding whether or not a specialty you would like to list is covered under medical necessity, you should either clarify that with the M.C.O. or delete that choice in favor of a specialization that is unquestionably covered.

OTHER APPLICATION SECTIONS

There are several other sections of the application that can have an affect upon the number of referrals you receive. These include length of treatment percentages, appointment availability, hospital privileges, and treatment philosophy.

Length of Treatment Percentages

Sometimes, M.C.O.s will ask about your average length of treatment percentages. This may appear within the application or on a separate sheet. Typically, this will be a series of questions such as the following:

In the past year, what percent of your patients completed treatment in:

# of Weeks:	Percentage
5 weeks or less	_____
6 to 10 weeks	_____
11 to 20 weeks	_____
21 weeks or more	_____

Be careful about how you answer this. If you have a significant percentage of patients whose treatment has exceeded 10 weeks, some M.C.O.s will feel that your philosophy of treatment is probably incompatible with their short-term model and may reject you on that basis. If you see a number of your patients once every other week or once a month, you should delineate that in one of two ways: (1) write in an explanatory note, or (2) cross out the word "weeks" and substitute the word "sessions" or "visits" and answer on that basis.

If you are seeing some patients intensively in order to keep them out of the hospital, then you are providing a service that most M.C.O.s highly value. Yet, unless you are careful in answering this question, the M.C.O. may penalize you for it, because your answer may be interpreted as an indication of a treatment philosophy biased toward long-term care. Therefore, definitely clarify that the purpose of those visits is to keep people out of the hospital. One way to do that is to add a separate, written-in category of "Patients treated intensively to keep them out of the hospital" and provide a percentage for that. If intensive outpatient treatment to alleviate the need for inpatient treatment is a specialty of yours, definitely list it as a specialty on your application.

Appointment Availability

Most M.C.O.s look for two things regarding appointment availability:

1. the shortest possible time between referral and first appointment, and
2. some evening or weekend hours.

It is not unusual for a managed care company to designate the speed with which patients can begin their treatment as one of the quality characteristics they emphasize in their own marketing to potential corporate accounts. When that situation exists, the M.C.O. keeps detailed track of time between initial intake calls to therapists and date of first treatment appointment. This record-keeping is a part of provider profiling that will be discussed in the next chapter.

Managed care companies usually prefer to refer to therapists who can offer an initial appointment within 24 hours. Since M.C.O.s book most of their business through contracts with employers, most of the potential patients are employees (though many are also dependents). Therefore, M.C.O.s definitely prefer to refer to therapists who offer evening appointments, weekend appointments, or both. If your application reflects an unwillingness to offer either evening or weekend appointments at least for a few hours on a regular basis each week, you may not be considered to be a serious referral point by the M.C.O.

Hospital Privileges

Applications often carry questions about hospital privileges even for some M.C.O.s who rarely use outpatient therapists for inpatient work. It is a good idea to list your hospital staff or affiliate staff privileges for three reasons:

1. This is sometimes used as a screening device to determine which therapists in the community are serious,
2. Quality-based managed care companies wish to ensure that their outpatient providers can coordinate care or follow clients inpatient when that is needed for continuity of care, and

3. Some M.C.O.s draw their inpatient panels (especially psychiatrists) from their general preferred provider lists.

For all of these reasons you should list *each* of the hospitals where you hold staff privileges or affiliate staff privileges. Listing each of them is important because you will get hospital-based referrals only for those hospitals that have contracts with the M.C.O. You will rarely be able to determine which hospitals have contracted with that managed care company. And it is quite common for an M.C.O. to change the hospitals it utilizes over very brief periods of time.

Treatment Philosophy

One of the questions M.C.O.s frequently ask on their applications has to do with treatment philosophy. There are several "right" answers to this question. And that is good because most therapists who have been in practice for some time tend to become pragmatists — borrowing from whatever therapeutic school appears to have an effective answer for a given situation. Therefore, most experienced clinicians can claim at least some experience in utilizing the treatment philosophy of a variety of schools of therapy.

If you have some knowledge and comfort with behavioral, cognitive, or systems theoretical orientations, do note that. Behavioral therapy is especially appreciated by some M.C.O.s because they try to define their recommended treatments by what has been shown by the literature to work. Behavioral researchers have published a large body of work regarding therapeutic techniques that is defensible on the basis of statistical validation. While some of the other schools of therapy have substantial publication to back up their concepts, their records tend to be more anecdotal in nature.

If you define yourself primarily as a psychoanalyst, you may find that many M.C.O.s will be less welcoming to you. This is because many M.C.O.s tend to see psychoanalysis as a very long-term treatment modality (in spite of the fact that Freud spoke of treating several patients with what we would probably now call brief therapy). If you specialize in psychoanalysis but would still like to work with M.C.O.s, you might want to consider some of the psychoanalytic theorists who utilize brief psychoanalysis. If you are comfortable with that orientation, use it on your application. But emphasize that you utilize *brief* psychoanalysis. And you will probably find it useful to go into some detail regarding the treatment philosophy, the clinicians and/or authors identified with the philosophy, and how it works for you.

The name which is probably most frequently associated with brief psychoanalysis is that of H. Davanloo.[1] A rather well-known videotape of his work is available and it illustrates his style fairly well. Others who tend toward a psychoanalytic use of brief therapy include M. Balint et al.,[2] S. Grand et al.,[3] and B. W. Tilley.[4] You may also wish to consider the works of David Malan[5] and P. E. Sifneos.[7]

NONAPPLICATION-BASED REFERRAL DEVELOPMENT

Although the application is usually the most important tool for referral development, it is definitely not the only one. And your referral development efforts should not be limited to the application. Every contact with a case manager should be considered a potential referral development opportunity. Announcement cards can often be helpful for both continuing name recognition and new service referrals. Provider newsletters should be perused for referral development opportunities. And M.C.O.-sponsored provider training should ALWAYS be attended both for knowledge development and referral development.

The next chapter is concerned with the third marketing challenge— Retention on the active panel. We will discuss the use of quality treatment and case manager relationships for long-term retention. As noted at the beginning of this chapter, the concepts we will be discussing will help with initial referral development as well as with follow-up referral development.

NOTES

1. Davanloo, H. (Ed.). *Basic Principles and Techniques in Short-term Dynamic Psychotherapy.* New York: Spectrum Publications, 1978 and Davanloo, H. (Ed.). *Short-term Dynamic Psychotherapy.* New York: J. Aronson, 1980.
2. Balint, M., Ornstein, P.H., & Balint, E. *Focal Psychotherapy: An Example of Applied Psychoanalysis.* London: Tavistock Publications Limited, 1972.
3. Grand, S., Rechetnick, J., Podrug, D., and Schwager, E. *Transference in Brief Psychotherapy: An Approach to the Study of Psychoanalytic Process.* Hillsdale, N.J.: Analytic Press, 1985.
4. Tilley, B. W. *Short-term Counseling: A Psychoanalytic Approach.* New York: International Universities Press, 1984.
5. Malan, D. H. *A Study of Brief Psychotherapy.* St. Louis, Missouri: Warren H. Green, 1970.
   Malan, D. H. *The Frontier of Brief Psychotherapy.* New York: Plenum, 1976.
6. Sifneos, P.E. *Short-term Psychotherapy and Emotional Crisis.* Cambridge, Massachusetts: Harvard University Press, 1972 and Sifneos, P.E. *Short-term Dynamic Psychotherapy: Evaluation and Technique.* New York: Plenum Medical Book Company, 1979.

5/
The Third Marketing Challenge: Retention on the Active Panel

Even after one gets accepted on a managed care organization's preferred provider panel and then obtains a stream of referrals, the marketing challenges are not over. Therapists must continue to market through providing an extremely high quality of service in order to stay on the list of clinicians who are actively utilized by each managed care organization.

As noted in Chapter 2, it is advantageous for an M.C.O. to demonstrate a very large provider network when the M.C.O. submits a bid for a contract with a corporation or large employer. Therefore, a managed care company may sign as many as 1,000 contracts with local therapists even if its primary corporate contract could be quite adequately serviced with only 250 therapists. This leaves the M.C.O. with an oversupply of contracted therapists. The oversupply problem gets redressed through provider culling at a later time.

Increasingly, a pattern is emerging of M.C.O.s culling their panels of preferred providers during the second and third years after major corporate contracts have been signed. It makes sense for the M.C.O.s to reduce their active list of preferred providers down to a figure closer to the number of therapists they actually need to service their contracts. The reduced administrative burden resulting from constricting provider lists can translate into substantial cost savings for the M.C.O.s.

Beyond that, M.C.O.s are aware that their product is a service. And the providers are the ones who deliver that service. The M.C.O. can compete for business in a variety of ways. The competition for business among M.C.O.s so far has focused primarily upon cost reduction. Bottom-line costs fall within a relatively narrow range and some M.C.O.s are beginning to focus primarily upon value for their competitive edge (see Chapter 6).

The value-driven M.C.O.s have a strong incentive to cull their lists of preferred providers. This makes it possible for the M.C.O. to work intensively with the small group of therapists who are retained for active utilization. With a small provider group the M.C.O. can get to know its contracted therapists well—including the strengths and weaknesses of each. Then clients can truly be directed to the therapists who are best for them. And some value-driven M.C.O.s are already joining with selected therapists in developing ongoing training. Thus, a truly high-quality provider network is beginning to be developed by selected M.C.O.s.

One of the steps in that process consists of culling the provider network. And a primary tool for network contraction is provider profiling. The fact that provider profiling has become a standard for quality improvement was verified in early 1992 by Joe Onek, a Washington attorney from Crowell & Moring specializing in health care issues, who said, "I think the new push in this field is going to be provider profile. . .(and other techniques) to find out who are the providers who do a quality (job)".[1]

PROVIDER PROFILES

Almost immediately after M.C.O.s begin actively servicing contracts in any geographic region, they usually begin tracking their levels of satisfaction with preferred providers through provider profiling. Ultimately, the provider profiles are utilized as one of the mechanisms for deciding how to reduce the active preferred provider list to a figure closer to the number of therapists the M.C.O.s actually need to service their contracts. Of course, those therapists who have most effectively met the needs of the managed care organization are the ones who are kept on the active list. In many cases only a minority of the therapists from the original preferred provider list are retained while the majority of therapists are cut from the active list. Managed care companies rarely make their cuts official. They simply focus upon referring to therapists who are on their active lists.

It is nearly impossible to extrapolate from one M.C.O.'s policies to another's. That is particularly true of provider profiling. Some companies deny that they engage in provider profiling at all. Others do it only very unofficially and superficially. M.C.C. of California, Inc. does it quite officially, meeting with selected providers and sharing the results of the individual therapist's statistical information collected from experience with the health plan's patients.

Most M.C.O.s are reluctant to disclose their data even if they admit to provider profiling. But the information available suggests that the majority of M.C.O.s that profile therapists consider a combination of a managed care-friendly attitude, sensitivity to the need for efficient treatment, good clinical skills, use of appropriate levels of treatment, skill in differential diagnosis, collegial interactions with case managers, clear and timely documentation, and sensitivity to the M.C.O.'s position in the marketplace. For example, one clinical observer, Elizabeth Horton, M.S.W., B.C.D., a member of the National Federation of Societies for Clinical Social Work's managed care committee, says that managed care companies identify high quality providers by their willingness to collaborate with the managed care process, their clients' improvement at a reasonable pace, and their clients' positive feedback to the networks.[2]

A QUALITY-BASED MARKETING PLAN

Some M.C.O.s market themselves exclusively on the basis of cost containment. Those M.C.O.s will skip quality criteria and focus only on cost criteria in their provider profiling. In the next chapter, we will look at why it will be to your advantage to avoid M.C.O.s that are driven exclusively by cost-containment criteria. On the other hand, a self-initiated quality plan will position you well for the value-driven managed care companies which will be your best partners. It will also begin to position you for the changes that are beginning to occur in this industry (see Chapter 7).

One of the M.C.O.s that is consistently ranked by providers as high quality and value-driven is Preferred Healthcare. Alex R. Rodriguez, M.D. is the chief medical officer and senior vice president of professional services for Preferred Healthcare. In a comment similar to that of Claire Ginger Wilson's (see Chapter 1), he notes that "therapy is moving from a trade to a business."[3] In a talk at the National Managed Health Care Congress on April 13, 1993, Dr. Rodriguez presented a slide developed by Kathleen Jennison Goonan, M.D., which contrasts the "trade" of psychotherapy with the "business" of managed behavioral health care. He notes that "These are characteristics of managed care systems, compared with traditional freedom-of-choice health care systems, to which practitioners will need to make accommodations":

TRADE	MANAGED CARE
Independent clinical judgements	Clinical treatment norms and protocols
Refer freely	Limit referrals
Inform patients of their decisions	Make decisions jointly with the patients
Become known as highly respected do-gooders	Are fallible
Are small businesspeople	Sell their expertise
Utilize individual billing	Utilize information systems[4]

Marketing professionals suggest that one of the best marketing strategies is to anticipate the client's needs and meet them. If one considers the business characteristics of managed care systems outlined by Dr. Goonan and combines them with the provider profiling criteria we discussed above, a framework emerges around which one can construct a quality-based marketing strategy that gives managed care companies what they want and need on a proactive basis. The following concepts are gleaned from a variety of sources so as to present a coherent, integrated service product that goes beyond just meeting provider profiling criteria to quietly, effectively, and proactively market you to any M.C.O. on the basis of quality. Because this plan goes well beyond the quality minimums that M.C.O.s require for active status retention, it should place you among the minority of therapists who are retained on any M.C.O.'s active list, except those utilizing non-quality criteria.

This plan consists of six elements: (1) attitude, (2) benefit sophistication, (3) demonstration of quality through practice structure, (4) demonstration of quality through clinical skills, (5) demonstration of quality through documentation, and (6) demonstration of quality through continuous improvement.

1. Attitude

The first component should be a familiarity with each M.C.O.'s treatment philosophy and some acceptance of such elements as brief therapy for selected disorders. There may well be some M.C.O.s that hold a treatment philosophy counter to yours. You should turn down contracts with them! The issue of choosing M.C.O. partners will be discussed in full detail in the next chapter. Here, suffice it to say that there are good and bad M.C.O.s just like most institutions. Because most M.C.O.s have instituted procedures that we sometimes feel impinge upon our patients rights — or our own — and because there are some M.C.O.s that are less ethical than they should be, we have a tendency to become skeptical of all M.C.O.s.

That skepticism was brought home to me when I mentioned to some colleagues that I was writing a book on managed care. One of them asked, "What's the name of it? Jaws?" Although he said a great amount in that small question, he is a man who tempers his deserved skepticism toward less ethical M.C.O.s with a positive, reality-based attitude toward value-based companies.

It is important for you also to keep your skepticism long enough to evaluate the quality of different M.C.O.s and then to acknowledge those deserving of a good attitudinal response from you. If you are unclear about a managed care company's philosophy, you can usually understand it by reading their mission statement and their protocols. If you are still unclear, talk to the medical director, because the implementation of that philosophy is directed by him.

There are two reasons M.C.O.s are extremely concerned about therapists' attitudes:

1. An attitude of shared commitment to the same goals insures far better functioning and promotes self-initiated quality efforts on the part of subcontractors. Toyota Motor Company has demonstrated to the world how important this concept is.

2. The clinician's attitude can easily get conveyed to patients, even when there is a conscious effort not to. And clients can bring that back to their employers (the M.C.O.'s primary customers). An attitude that this M.C.O.'s policies promote effective, relatively fair arrangements for ensuring maintenance of employer-sponsored behavioral health care ultimately benefits the M.C.O. when it gets back to the employer. Less favorable attitudes ultimately cause problems for the M.C.O. when they get back to the employer.

The effect of attitude on internal functioning becomes especially apparent when it comes to interactions between therapists and M.C.O. case managers. In the better M.C.O.s, case managers are extremely well trained and can work collegially with therapists for the patient's benefit. When it works well, this is like having a consultant on call; my own experience is that it often results in better treatment. Several case managers I have worked with have coordinated treatment when multiproblem families have gone to numerous therapists and had a variety of partial and full hospitalizations.[5] With one M.C.O. I have had a series of particularly difficult cases (we all have runs of difficult cases occasionally), and the case manager has constructively problem-solved with me over and over.[6]

Case managers have also kept track of the total number of visits available to patients under their employer's contract and have worked out appropriate care arrangements, thus ensuring that the patient does not have unnecessary out-of-pocket expenses.[7] And they have even substituted inpatient days for outpatient days to provide more appropriate coverage.[8]

All of these efforts and more contribute to a collegial service mode that makes it easy for me to be enthusiastic about the role of case managers. Most of us who have been in private practice probably have an inclination to become defensive, especially when someone neither we nor the patient has ever met suggests an alternative to the procedures we propose. But, except when the alternative suggestions do not appear to be in the patient's best interest, it makes sense to get past the defensiveness and see if something valuable is available.

This means seriously CONSIDERING alternative treatment suggestions and discussing them within a collegial framework. It does not necessarily mean that the M.C.O.s expect universal agreement with the positions of the case managers. In most cases, you can appeal the case manager's decisions and as long as that is done in a businesslike manner with good documentation for your position, it will not be seen as a negative on your profile — in fact many would probably see that as a positive. With value-based managed care companies, particularly, you will probably find that most of the case managers will offer valuable help. The fact that M.C.O.s usually include information about the clinician's attitude toward case managers in their provider rating makes sense, because a constructive attitude often constitutes the critical component in determining whether or not the case management process works well.

2. Benefit Sophistication

Helping your patients understand and come to terms with their changed benefit structures is not written into our positions with managed care companies. But therapists are often the ones who end up with that task. And since we are the ones with face-to-face patient contact, we are sometimes the best positioned for this task. Managed care companies sell their service products to corporate employers. The corporations often reduce benefits at the same time they contract with a managed care company. But the M.C.O. is left to explain this fact to the employees while at the same time trying to create a good impression with both the employees and their corporate employer. This effort to make a good impression is especially important if the M.C.O.'s contract will soon be up for renewal.

Managed care companies appreciate therapist sensitivity to this frequently contradictory position they hold in the marketplace. Since clients often do not understand (and sometimes do not read) their benefit booklets, it is frequently left to therapists to explain things such as why the contract calls for up to 50 visits but those can only be utilized if authorized or why visits will only be authorized if they are deemed to be medically necessary. If you take the time to understand these benefit restrictions and the rationale for them and then go further to find ways to explain this to patients in clear, nonjudgmental ways, you will eventually earn the appreciation of the patients, the employers, and the M.C.O.s.

Neal Andrews, who has held several prominent positions in behavioral managed care, has noted that "What is sold is insurance; not entitlement. Managed care companies' contracts do not provide treatment on the basis of guaranteed coverage for a certain number of visits. Often therapists communicate to patients that the patients' employer has paid for 50 visits and therefore the client should get 50 visits. What they paid for was to participate in a pool of people who may or may not need 50 visits and the maximum exposure per case is limited to 50 visits. But the price is set on the expectation that only around 3% to 5% of the pool will need any services and that the average number of visits needed will be less than 10."[9] It can sometimes be helpful to aid the patient in seeing that this kind of actuarial-based benefit structure is what makes it possible to keep his insurance premiums from increasing even faster than they already are.

Medical necessity is another term that arises out of the insurance-based structure of the managed care industry. Many M.C.O.s are owned by insurance companies and utilize traditional insurance yardsticks to determine what is covered and what is not. M.C.O.s will only reimburse for treatment that is felt to be "medically necessary" for the relief of symptoms or conditions as defined by the D.S.M. However, the definition of medical necessity differs from one M.C.O. to another and sometimes from one M.C.O. contract to another. Finding out what is covered under medical necessity is desirable for two reasons:

1. So that you can explain to the patient why certain services cannot be reimbursable, saving the patient from possibly incurring a nonreimbursable cost and allowing him or her to make an informed choice about whether or not to contract for the service on a fee-for-service basis.
2. So that the therapist does not treat for an unbillable service which he or she discovers is unbillable only when the claim comes back rejected.

Often, patients complete the work they initially come in to do and then wish to stay in treatment to deal with additional issues which may not meet the criteria of medical necessity. When that happens, most M.C.O. contracts allow the therapist to point out that the additional service is nonreimbursable and can be contracted for on an out-of-pocket basis if the patient wants to do that. Of course, the care with which this gets explained will go a long way toward preserving good feelings toward the managed care company by this patient. Neal Andrews explains how coverage works in this way: "Managed care companies typically sell coverage for problem-oriented modalities and services. . . . For example, we usually don't cover personality restructuring (which in many cases is considered medically necessary by the DSM-III), self-realization programs, or self-improvement counselling services."[10]

This explanation of benefits and the fit between what is covered by insurance benefits and what must be covered on an out-of-pocket basis if the patient wants it is similar to the discussions most of us are used to having with our clients regarding Axis V code diagnoses when the patients were utilizing indemnity insurance. Such discussions became standard and common when patients thought they could utilize their behavioral health insurance for marital counselling and had to be told that it was nonreimbursable since marital counselling is an Axis V code diagnosis. Since most therapists are accustomed to this kind of discussion from our work with V codes, it is a service we are fairly well equipped to provide. And it is a service that most M.C.O.s will appreciate our providing.

3. Demonstrating Quality Through Practice Structure

There are several ways your practice can be structured so as to enhance your value to M.C.O.s. Some evening and/or weekend hours are critical. An ability to respond to a crisis quickly is usually appreciated and sometimes required. This may mean a live answering service with call-forwarding capability or it may mean utilizing a beeper. Most managed care people I have spoken with prefer that you use an answering machine for most message retrieval in non-crisis situations, so that callers can quickly leave a detailed message without the possibility that it will get distorted. You will also find case managers often expressing their appreciation if you can find a way to print, type, or computerize your reports so that they can be easily read. You will find, too, that a tickler file or calendar is critical to meeting various M.C.O. reporting deadlines. And the degree to which you are consistent in meeting deadlines is noted by most M.C.O.s. (Often, it is noted on your provider profile.)

Some familiarity with the structure and history of managed care, but especially the economic rationale for managed care, is often appreciated. M.C.O.s also usually prefer therapists who maintain membership in their state or national professional associations since those organizations promote professionalism and help therapists keep aware of both marketplace and treatment trends. That awareness makes it possible for the therapist to anticipate the needs of M.C.O.s. And sometimes it relieves M.C.O.s of the necessity for long explanations about changes.

4. Demonstrating Quality Through Clinical Skills

Superior patient care is the primary mechanism by which a therapist can market himself on the basis of quality. Dr. Peter Sterman, Regional Director of Provider Systems for Preferred Health Care, Ltd. has noted the following traits his organization considers to be important:

Ability to perform comprehensive assessments,
Ability to develop a comprehensive and focused treatment plan,
Ability to be aggressive (in resolving) diagnostic ambiguity, and
Ability to assess discharge planning issues.[11]

One of the points Dr. Sterman's listing highlights is that measurements for quality are concrete, specific, and pragmatic with managed care. The criteria that suggest quality under indemnity insurance vary because they are defined by the values underlying each therapist's theoretical orientation. This difference in the definition of quality occurs partly because the patient was seen as the exclusive client under indemnity insurance, while managed care sees the primary purchaser—the insurance company, employer, or governmental body—as another client to be considered. Thus, efficiency and accountability are extremely important components of quality care. The following are the elements that most managed care companies would consider to be essential for quality-based patient care:

1. Comprehensive assessments:

   This should include the normal assessment criteria with a differential diagnosis (including a chemical dependency screening), and an emphasis on relapse history, community resources, and discharge planning. In most cases, the M.C.O. will have already screened for possible inpatient criteria. Nevertheless, you should, of course, do a re-screening of whether the patient is a danger to self or others.

2. Aggressive resolution of any diagnostic ambiguity.

3. Protocols for early problem identification.

4. Consistent links between symptoms, diagnosis, treatment plans, progress reports, closing report, and Axis V ratings.

   Diagnosis should be based on symptomatology and treatment plans should address that same symptomatology. At each stage (diagnosis, each progress report, and closing), Axis V should be consistent with the level of symptomatology or progress reported. For example, it is infrequent (but not exactly rare) that a patient will experience treatment progress along with a lower Axis V level of functioning. When that does occur, it should be explained in the report.

5. Utilization of aggressive brief treatment approaches, unless there are clear indications that an alternative approach is preferable.

   When an alternative approach is used, the rationale should be documented. Aggressive brief therapy means finding a treatment focus and avoiding extraneous issues to the degree that is appropriately possible. The treatment approach should be validated by the literature, usual and customary, and diagnosis-specific. Later in this chapter, in the discussion of demonstrating quality through continuous improvement, we will discuss the importance of specializing in order to keep up with the research and literature so that one can stay current on what the most effective treatment approach is. And in Chapter 7, we will discuss the trend toward establishing benchmark methodologies to develop preferred treatment approaches as well as guidelines for diagnostic-specific treatment. When there is evidence that a particular approach has been validated, you should utilize it or note in your records why you have chosen not to.

6. Level-of-care guidelines that are least restrictive.

   The therapist should be familiar with criteria for each level of care, including: inpatient, partial hospitalization, day treatment, alternative treatment centers, community residential centers, intensive outpatient, and weekly outpatient psychotherapy. This will make it possible to determine the most appropriate level of care, which is usually the one that meets the patient's needs at the least restrictive level. For example, inpatient care should not be selected if structured day treatment programs will work equally well.

7. Treatment justification within the context of the contracted benefits.

   Requests for additional treatment should always be accompanied by appropriate justifications based upon current symptomatology, concurrent Axis V level of functioning, treatment progress or lack of it, and new or continuing barriers to progress. Treatment should always be to acuity. In the past, some clinicians—especially in inpatient centers—treated the patient until insurance ran out and then discharged. Although this was uncommon, it tarnished the behavioral health care industry and led to substantial sensitivity on the part of payers about the need to justify length of stay on the part of both inpatient and outpatient programs. When there are disagreements, M.C.O.s are insistent that clients be sheltered from them. And they get even more upset when personnel departments are pulled into disputes.

8. Use of specialized treatment groups whenever that is possible and desirable for an individual patient's care.

9. Consultation on both an as-needed and random basis.

   If you are in a group practice, regular collegial reviews and expert clinician reviews are desirable.

10. Extensive and documented utilization of community resources, especially peer groups.

    Although 12-step groups are not the only kind of community peer group to refer to, they should certainly be included. I keep schedules of about 10 kinds of community resources (usually peer groups) and 10 kinds of 12-step meetings, which I hand out to clients on an as-needed basis. Community peer groups can constitute an excellent support and supplement to therapy. And often they provide a good framework around which to build a discharge plan.

Many studies validate that attendance in 12-step self-help groups is critical for patients in recovery for substance abuse. In one, a 1988 study conducted by Parkside Medical Services Corporation, head-quartered in Park Ridge, Illinois, patients with just primary treatment (outpatient, residential treatment center-based, and hospital-based were all studied) were compared to those who had completed a program that included self-help group attendance. They found a 22% increase in effectiveness with those who attended the self-help groups.[12] Community resource referrals should always be made a part of the treatment plan when possible and the referrals should always be documented, even when patients fail to comply. Sophistication in the use of community resources demonstrates to managed care personnel that you structure treatment within the context of the patient's overall resources, with a goal of maximum effectiveness.

11. Use of multi-specialty approaches and consultation.

This is another aspect of structuring therapy within the context of external resources, utilizing multi-specialty professional skills. It is important to consistently get an evaluation for medication if there is any indication it would be useful. This should always be done as early in treatment as possible, preferably after the first or second session. Early medication evaluation can result in medication choice and level setting concurrent with outpatient therapy, so that the therapist can provide the psychiatrist with direct observational feedback regarding the effects of the different kinds and levels of medications. Too often, when brief therapy is undertaken, the patient concludes his psychotherapy before it has been possible to determine the most appropriate kind and dosage of medication.

12. Utilize homework and bibliotherapy.

Outside assignments increase your effectiveness and clients' motivation. When these are utilized, patients become involved in their own treatment for longer than just the therapy session each week. As a result, they usually progress faster. You should document your use of these tools on your treatment plans, because most managed care personnel love to see this kind of intensive, proactive treatment. This kind of work with a client can also alert you to compliance issues. If the client is noncompliant, it can be useful to determine whether or not the noncompliance is a manifestation of resistance and — if so — what can be done with that. Document your conclusions because this dynamic may constitute an indicator of the need for longer term intervention.

13. Understand the managed care company's utilization management criteria and proactively work to meet those guidelines.

Some M.C.O.s do not share their criteria, but after you have sent in a few reports (especially treatment plans) and received some responses, you will probably be able to extrapolate a great deal of information about guidelines.

5. Demonstrating Quality Through Documentation

Documentation offers the primary mechanism by which managed care personnel can track quality. Thus, it also should be addressed proactively by the quality-based clinician so as to ensure that documentation is done in such a way that it anticipates and exceeds the M.C.O.'s expectations. Documentation needs to be current, complete, and geared to the special needs of each M.C.O.—frequently even to each corporate contract held by the M.C.O. Following are recommendations for quality documentation:

1. Office policies—especially no-show policies—should be documented, and you should request that clients sign an acknowledgement of having read them.
2. A tickler file or other calendaring device should be utilized to ensure that all reports are completed on time.
3. You may find it helps to write out the reporting procedures (including which forms are necessary) for each of the M.C.O.s you work with, so that each gets what it needs in a timely manner. I find this an invaluable help.
4. Maintain records of each treatment session. This will be very helpful when making periodic reports. It is also important should a question come up later regarding why you did or did not utilize a particular procedure.
5. While originating records, keep in mind that all of your records will be available to future retrospective reviewers, and document accordingly. The rationale for each important clinical decision should be documented to the degree that is realistically possible.
6. **ALWAYS** keep copies of all of your records. A photocopier can be an excellent investment.
7. As noted previously, try to keep records legible. Reports should be printed, typed, or originated on a computer.

6. Demonstrating Quality Through Continuous Improvement

One of the most important components of a quality-based marketing plan should consist of procedures for continuous improvement. In Chapter 7 we will be discussing the new continuous quality improvement processes, which are a part of the near-future trends in the behavioral managed health care picture. On an individual level, therapists can prepare for and anticipate the emphasis that will soon be placed upon this. Two continuous quality improvement components are critical: continuing education and T.Q.M. (total quality management).

Therapists have always been aware of the need to pursue continuing education, but it is even more critical under the rigors of managed care. Education regarding managed care itself (such as reading this book) is very much appreciated by most M.C.O.s. Developing additional education or skills in any of the above-listed quality components should be useful to you and valued by M.C.O.s. The explosion of knowledge regarding dynamics and treatment procedures for most of the DSM diagnoses makes continuing education imperative for those therapists who wish to provide state-of-the-art quality treatment to their patients.

This exponential increase in the knowledge base of our field suggests that therapists will soon be forced to specialize in narrow areas just because that will be the only way to stay current in the most effective treatments for any given diagnosis. And M.C.O.s are increasingly expecting therapists to be able to justify their treatment techniques on the basis of most-effective-treatment research. Continuing education will increasingly become necessary to understand what those most-effective-treatment regimes are and for developing the justification base that will be a part of both concurrent and retrospective reviews.

Value-based managed care companies consider T.Q.M. (total quality management) to be a component critical to their market niche. Total quality management is a mechanism for continuous improvement through the monitoring and measuring of quality of care. Although individually therapists cannot take on a big research project, there are several relatively simple quality feedback mechanisms that will position an individual provider to increase his value to quality-driven managed care organizations. You can do your own customer satisfaction surveys by asking clients to complete a questionnaire at the conclusion of their treatment. You can also do a simplified outcome measurement through conducting pre- and post-tests of patient symptomatology. And you can also monitor your own quality through paying attention on a programmed, continuous basis to the quality measures discussed here. One way you as an individual therapist can ensure continuous quality is to utilize a quality checklist and periodically check your performance on each item. The above components have been compiled together here for such a checklist:

QUALITY CHECKLIST

The following is a therapist personal quality checklist that should help you implement a quality-based marketing approach:

Attitude:
1. Familiarity with treatment philosophy. _____
2. Interactions with case managers. _____

Benefit sophistication:
3. Understanding contract benefit structure. _____
4. Capability of explaining benefit structure. _____
5. Benefit entitlement counselling capability. _____
6. Medical necessity understanding. _____
7. Medical necessity explanation & counselling capability. _____

Practice structure:
8. Evening / weekend hours. _____
9. Crisis response capability. _____
10. Clear message retrieval capability (answering machine?). _____
11. Emergency coverage. _____
12. Report consistency of ease-of-reading (printing?) of reports. _____
13. Deadlines consistency (tickler file?). _____
14. State professional affiliation. _____

Clinical Skills:
Comprehensive assessments
15. Inclusive. _____

Early problem identification:
16. Presenting problem. _____
17. Identification of recent life changes. _____
18. Identification of probable treatment focus. _____
19. Chemical dependency screening. _____
20. Relapse history (if appropriate). _____
21. Past treatment. _____
22. Patient history. _____

23. History of family of origin. _____
24. Extended family and community resources. _____
25. Discharge planning criteria. _____
26. Resolution of diagnostic ambiguity. _____

Clinical linking consistency:
27. Symptomatology—Diagnosis. _____
28. Symptomatology—Treatment plans. _____
29. Symptomatology—Progress reports. _____
30. Symptomatology—Closing report. _____
31. Symptomatology—Axis V. _____
32. Diagnosis—Treatment plans. _____
33. Diagnosis—Progress reports. _____
34. Diagnosis—Closing report. _____
35. Diagnosis—Axis V. _____
36. Treatment plans—Progress reports. _____
37. Treatment plans—Closing report. _____
38. Treatment plans—Axis V. _____
39. Progress reports—Closing report. _____
40. Progress reports—Axis V. _____
41. Closing report—Axis V. _____

Appropriate treatment:
42. Brief. _____
43. Focused. _____
44. Validated by the literature. _____
45. Usual and customary. _____
46. Diagnostic-specific. _____
47. Most effective (when known). _____
48. Least restrictive level of care. _____
49. Treatment to acuity. _____
50. Discharge criteria within initial treatment plan. _____
51. Use of specialized treatment groups. _____

Consultation or treatment review:
52. Consultation. _____
53. Managed care case manager utilization review. _____
54. Group practice scheduled U.R. (Collegial). _____
55. Group practice scheduled U.R. (Expert clinician). _____
56. Group practice random U.R. (Collegial). _____
57. Group practice random U.R. (Expert clinician). _____
58. Utilization of community peer groups (12-step, etc.). _____

Multi-specialty consultation/referral:
59. Referral for medication evaluation (when indicated). _____
60. Referral for testing (when indicated). _____

Treatment Session Extensions:
61. Use of homework assignments. _____
62. Bibliotherapy. _____
63. Understanding of M.C.O.'s utilization management criteria. _____
64. Proactive stance to meet utilization management criteria. _____

Documentation: _____
65. Office policy documentation with client signature. _____
66. Calendaring of report deadlines. _____
67. Reporting procedure worksheet. _____
68. Individual treatment session records. _____
69. Documentation for retrospective reviews. _____
70. Long-term record retention. _____
71. Legible records. _____

Total Quality Management:
72. Continuing education. _____
73. Pre-test given. _____
74. Post-test given. _____
75. Analysis of pre- and post-test results. _____
76. Customer satisfaction survey. _____

SUMMARY

In this chapter we have considered the desirability of marketing one's private practice on the basis of quality. We have looked at the increased need and viability of that in light of provider profiling. Then a quality-based marketing plan was presented, which encompassed (1) attitude, (2) benefit sophistication, (3) demonstrating quality through practice structure, (4) clinical skills, (5) documentation, and (6) continuous improvement. Finally, a quality checklist was presented reflecting items from all of the quality characteristics.

Even though as an individual therapist some of these quality mechanisms may be a stretch for you, it makes sense to begin to implement as many as possible as soon as possible. In that way, you can position yourself to become the kind of therapist who is in demand by value-based M.C.O.s.

By doing this and utilizing the other marketing strategies noted so far in this book, you can position yourself to have sufficient managed care provider opportunities that you can begin to pick and choose among managed care partners. Such choices are critical to long-term success and satisfaction!

In the next chapter we will be discussing how to make those critical partnership choices. In the chapter after that, we will return to the concept of quality, since it is critical to near-term changes that we can increasingly expect in the marketplace. But an added element will consist of the need to promote practice quality within the context of group provider practices. Many of the characteristics discussed here will gain added importance and sophistication as they graduate from elements in individual provider quality-based niches to become elements in provider group quality-based niches.

NOTES

1. Quote from "Mental Health Weekly," Vol 2, #4, dated 1/27/1992.
   Private communication in 7/91 with Mindy Inselberg of M.C.C. of California.
2. From quote in the *National Federation of Societies for Clinical Social Work, Inc. Progress Report*, 11/1992, Volume 10, #2. page 10.
3. Rodriguez, Alex R., M.D. In presentation to the National Managed Health Care Congress entitled, "Behavioral Health Providers: Negotiating 'Favorable Contracts' with M.C.O.s" on 4/13/93.
4. Material developed by Kathleen Jennison Goonan, M.D. and presented by Alex R. Rodriguez, M.D. to the National Managed Health Care Congress entitled, "Behavioral Health Providers: Negotiating 'Favorable Contracts' with M.C.O.s" on 4/13/93.
5. Linda DaRocha, L.C.S.W. of Preferred Health Care, Kathi Walsh, R.N. of U.S. Behavioral Health of California, and one other (see #6 below).
6. The legal department of this M.C.O. prefers to remain unidentified.
7. Cynthia Hunt-Smith, M.F.C.C. of M.C.C. of California and one other (see #6 above).
8. Kathi Walsh, R.N. of U. S. Behavioral Health and one other (see #6 above).
9. Private interview with Neal Andrews, on 10/13/92.
10. Private interview with Neal Andrews, on 10/13/92.
11. Peter Sterman, Ph.D., Regional director of provider systems for Preferred Health Care, Ltd. in a speech given to the San Fernando Valley Chapter of Employee Assistance Providers' Association on 10/01/91
12. Reported in *"Behavioral Health Industry Statistics, Monograph 42"* by John Krizay and Monica Oss published by Open Minds. April, 1991 Volume 4, Issue 1.

6/
Strategic Positioning: Targeting Your M.C.O. Partners

Marketing does not occur in a vacuum. It can help to see marketing as a tool, which can be utilized in a variety of ways. Implementation should be specific, thoughtful, planned, strategic, and goal-directed. Some kind of time element should be attached. (A time lag of one and one-half to two years often occurs between first contact with a managed care company that is new to a local area and the first stream of client referrals originating from that M.C.O.)

It is helpful to do both an initial marketing analysis and also an ongoing analysis since the behavioral health care delivery system marketplace is rapidly changing; new M.C.O. products are being developed continuously, and personnel are constantly changing. All of these changes can result in new opportunities as well as new obstacles for you. Beyond that, the desirability of contracting with any given M.C.O. should be reevaluated at various points, since some of the advantages and disadvantages of a given M.C.O. will not become apparent until after the therapist starts servicing patients who have been referred by that M.C.O., especially since M.C.O. policies are continuously being refined.

THE MOST IMPORTANT SUGGESTION: MAINTAIN YOUR OPTIONS!

Marketing should be directed. Some M.C.O.s are far more advantageous for the therapist to affiliate with than others. In fact, some can actually be toxic to the therapist's ethics, bottom line profitability, and/or legal security. Probably the most valuable suggestion I can give you regarding a strategic marketing plan is to market yourself in such a way that you can receive offers of preferred provider contracts from a wide variety of M.C.O.s so that you can become relatively comfortable in maintaining the options of declining or of deciding to contract while intending to remain relatively inactive.

The M.C.O.s you contract with will become your business partners in every legal, ethical, and functional aspect of that term. If you share offices with other therapists, you have probably checked out their reputations and taken various steps to ensure that you will be helped—or at least not harmed—by your relationship with those colleagues. And you probably have gone even further to ensure legal and financial protection if you have taken on business partners. The same care should be taken when considering M.C.O. contracts.

The M.C.O.s you contract with will become your partner in three important areas of your business:

1. the function of delivering your services to the client,
2. legal risks,
3. financial gains.

The delineation of how those risks and gains are shared and of how the function of providing therapy is undertaken will be spelled out in the contract, which constitutes your partnership agreement. Since the contract is written by attorneys specifically retained for that purpose by the M.C.O., all aspects of your partnership agreement will be on the M.C.O.'s terms — not yours. Your one choice is whether or not you wish to participate. Since the option to decline the contract is your only opportunity to protect yourself, please try to not limit it by a mind set that leaves you desperate for contracts.

Some therapists make two mistakes that compound each other when it comes to contracting with M.C.O.s. First, they wait until they are informed that an M.C.O. has signed a contract with the employer of some of their patients before they seek to become a preferred provider. As noted earlier, that is a sure path to rejection, since most provider networks are full by that point. Once the therapist has experienced several (or even one) of those rejections, he decides, "Never again," seeks out new M.C.O.s, and signs every contract he can get his hands on.

Signing every possible contract is foolish. Some M.C.O.s provide a fee to therapists that is so low it will not even offset the cost of office space plus the needed office help to process their paperwork. A few M.C.O.s include legal clauses in their contracts that force the therapist to risk his financial well-being in order to comply with the contract.

STRATEGIC GOAL:
A DIVERSIFIED PORTFOLIO

At the beginning of this chapter, I noted that strategic planning should be goal-directed. Formulating a goal means developing a picture of what the end result of the goal-directed process will be. In the present case this means developing a picture of the mix of M.C.O.s you want to work with. In formulating that goal, two overall concepts should be considered: diversification and quality.

Investment risk managers usually suggest diversification of financial investment portfolios. It makes sense to do the same thing with the portfolio of managed care contracts you begin to accumulate. You will probably find it helpful to try for a mix of very large companies and some smaller, local companies.

Probably the largest managed care company at this point is owned by Medco Behavioral Care Corporation. Due to recent buyouts, Medco now controls three previously separate managed care companies which were each fairly large to begin with: Assured, Biodyne, and Personal Performance Consultants. Other major managed care companies that are probably in the top 10 regarding enrollment are Preferred Health Care, Human Affairs International, Green Spring Health Services, M.C.C. Companies, and American PsychManagement.

All other things being equal it is especially important to include large M.C.O.s in your portfolio of contracts because of their present and future positions in the marketplace. In Chapter 7 we will be discussing trends in managed care. While there is repositioning and jockeying for market niches, another strong trend consists of consolidation. The probability is high that most of the M.C.O.s that ultimately come to dominate this market will emerge from those that presently hold large numbers of contracts. Large M.C.O.s are also safer for two reasons:

1. As consolidation occurs, a number of small — especially, regional —
   M.C.O.s are being purchased by larger corporations. When that
   happens, restructuring often follows, with many complications for the
   contracted providers.
2. The larger M.C.O.s are especially suited to respond effectively to
   managed competition. Monica Oss predicts that when managed
   competition (the American Health Security Act) is finally implemented, "We can expect to see the same players dominating the
   marketplace."[1]

On the other hand, working with small — especially, local — M.C.O.s can
be a genuine pleasure. It is easier to meet and to form more personal professional relationships with those in policy-making positions when you
contract with small, local companies. This can result in benefit flexibility
so that the ultimate clients (both the patients and the corporate employers)
are very well served.

Even as you seek to diversify your portfolio of managed care contracts,
you should keep in mind that you will be working in a way that is counter
to the strategic interests of many M.C.O.s — at least from the perspective of
their policy-makers. One of the reasons a number of M.C.O.s are seeking to
pare down their lists of active preferred providers is so that they can begin
to supply a patient referral flow that will ultimately be sufficient to constitute the greater part of their providers' practices.

In Chapter 7 we will discuss the fact that M.C.O.s are seeking to position
themselves in the marketplace through finding a niche. One of the primary
areas around which niches are being developed consists of a continuum
between those working exclusively for low cost at one end of the spectrum
and those positioning themselves on the basis of value (a combination of
cost containment and high quality) at the other end. The high-value M.C.O.s
can effectively be labelled as quality-based since that is the segment of value
that distinguishes them from low-cost companies. Both low-cost and
quality-based M.C.O.s emphasize cost containment.

It is very much to your advantage to focus upon a goal of working
exclusively — or at least primarily — with high-value M.C.O.s. This may not
be possible immediately. However, if you pursue your marketing effectively,
over time you can cull out the lower quality M.C.O.s and position your
practice primarily with high-value ones.

What is a high-value managed care company? An overview is provided
by a quote from Maureen Cardiff, M.S.W., B.C.D., a therapist who has

already positioned her practice primarily with high-value M.C.O.s. In a communication with Ian Shaffer, M.D., vice-president of medical affairs and chief medical officer of American PsychManagement, Inc., (quoted here by permission), Ms. Cardiff stated, "It maintains a professional relationship between provider and case manager with mutual respect. It demonstrates quality, cost-effective treatment for the patient. And it evidences a corporate attitude which validates and supports the patient, the provider and the case manager."[2] Throughout the rest of this chapter, we will be discussing details of how these qualities get played out in specifics that will allow you to evaluate whether or not to contract with a particular company.

You will find it extremely advantageous to avoid those M.C.O.s that seek to position themselves in the marketplace exclusively on the basis of low cost. The reason is that nearly every one of the mechanisms for implementing cost containment can be driven to excess and often is. When this happens, many legal, ethical, and financial problems can be created for the M.C.O.'s psychotherapist providers.

M.C.O.s can compete on the basis of cost only by cutting their own expenditures to the bone. Low-cost M.C.O.s often hire insufficiently trained staff in insufficient numbers. They compound this by making monetary-based clinical decisions. Many potential problems can result. When the therapist seeks to reach clinical staff of the M.C.O., it is frequently extremely difficult to find out whom to talk to, and it may be even more difficult to reach that person, who may be so far backed up that he or she realistically has little time for decision-making, much less for problem-solving. Consequently, the therapist may spend inordinate amounts of time just waiting on the phone and more time playing phone tag.

Once a decision is made, it may well be a clinically poor one that can result in poor patient care if implemented, thus compromising both the ethical and legal integrity of the therapist. The therapist may choose to appeal. However, there may be no appeal process, or the appeal process may exist in name only. I have even known of times when the managed care clinical personnel did not understand the dynamic structure of the illness and therefore made totally uninformed decisions—after consulting with the medical director! (To be fair, even with the most restrictive M.C.O.s this kind of conundrum is somewhat rare.) More frequently, clinical restrictions are based upon extreme limits in the M.C.O.-employer contract. Contract clauses that can result in poor patient care are usually avoided by the better quality-based M.C.O.s, if for no other reason than that their own internal risk management demands dropping the clauses.

Quick Screen

Another way low-cost M.C.O.s reduce their expenditures is through reducing provider reimbursement payments. Since there is a fairly direct correlation between low provider reimbursement levels and M.C.O.s that market themselves on a low-cost basis, this can be a quick way to screen for those companies best avoided. Set a reimbursement rate in your mind that you feel you can live with and that reflects the majority of managed care policies and refuse to contract below it. You will probably avoid the most dangerous companies.

Decision Points

Each time you receive a new contract, you will face three choices: (1) to contract with that M.C.O., (2) to decline to contract with that organization, or (3) to contract with the idea of maintaining an inactive status. There will be choice indicators at every step of the contracting process—and even beyond that into the implementation of the contract. In the majority of cases the most important decision point will be at the end of your contract analysis. This is the time to determine whether or not you can live with a contract with this M.C.O. There are some companies that are so bad you will decide not to proceed as soon as you hear about their reputation or see one of their advertisements. And you may find a number of marginal M.C.O.s.

As the foregoing chapters have indicated, you will probably have a limited window of opportunity to sign with a company before its preferred provider list closes. Therefore, if you are undecided about whether or not a particular M.C.O. will make a good business partner for you, it is often a better policy to go ahead and sign a contract with the thought that later you may decide to discontinue with that M.C.O. The decision to tentatively sign should be made only after first looking over the clauses that outline the notification lead time for quitting the contract, conditions for quitting the contract, and whether or not there are any penalties. (Usually there are none.)

The Inactive Status Choice

In most cases the criteria covered in this chapter will lead you to a definite decision regarding whether or not to contract with a given M.C.O. But there may be times when you will be unsure about the wisdom of contracting or of declining. This can occur under the following circumstances:

1. If your caseload has been fairly full for awhile with clients referred from M.C.O.s you like as partners, but you are unsure how long that will last.
2. If this M.C.O.'s reputation, quality, or provider fee schedule is marginal, and you need some experience to determine whether or not you can work comfortably with it.
3. If you would normally decline but you discover that this M.C.O. has a good chance of contracting with a major employer in your area.
4. If this company has recently been purchased or stands a good chance of merging with another M.C.O. whose quality is far better (or worse). This includes more M.C.O.s as time goes by.
5. If this M.C.O. is involved as a primary contractor to a regional purchasing cooperative under managed competition (the American Health Security Act)—or if it has a good chance of becoming involved as a primary contractor in the future. (Please see Chapter 8.)

When circumstances like these exist, you will probably still need to make a decision expeditiously, since provider contracting phases are of increasingly short duration and the provider list will probably close soon. If you get into this bind, you can often buy yourself time by contracting with an intent to remain as inactive as possible. M.C.O.s will usually understand if you have to (or choose to) decline to accept a few patients. But if you establish a pattern of declining all patients, you will probably be effectively (or officially) dropped from that M.C.O.'s preferred provider list. So this option is one that must be used carefully and only for a short period of time. If you do decide to utilize an inactive option, you should:

1. Write down for yourself what your reasons are.
2. Determine what steps need to be taken (or what needs to occur) to resolve your ambiguities.
3. Give yourself a time line for making a decision to decline or to become active with the M.C.O.

During the time you are inactive, you will be a listed provider but will simply decline all or most of the referrals you receive from the managed care company. Sometimes, "inactive" providers accept a few referrals to fill empty hours, but do not do any marketing to generate referrals. I suggest that you do this only with care. If there are problems with a company or a contract, you can usually expose yourself to them with even one referral.

Now let us discuss the choice considerations in each phase of the contracting/implementation process. A summary outline will be provided at the end of this chapter to give you a more condensed and convenient guide for evaluating M.C.O.s.

INVESTIGATION PHASE

In Chapter 2, we discussed the desirability of your becoming proactive in searching for new and expanding M.C.O.s in your local area. When undertaking that task, it is advisable to investigate the reputations of these companies. There are various ways to accomplish this. One of the best ways is to ask local employee assistance professionals. If the M.C.O. is starting to become active in your area through seeking contracts, E.A.P.s have probably become aware of it because E.A.P.s are often on the teams that evaluate managed care contract bids. And those E.A.P.s who are part of a national corporation may well know of the M.C.O.'s reputation in other geographic regions.

If the M.C.O. you are considering contracting with has been active in your area for any length of time at all, you will probably find it helpful to check with other therapists who have had experience with it. If the M.C.O. has been active in another region of the country, you can check with colleagues there as well as with national professional organizations.

Specialized behavioral health care newsletters can be particularly helpful to your efforts to investigate the reputations of companies new to your area. (See the listing of newsletters in Chapter 2.) Even when a M.C.O. is a totally new business venture, the newsletters and the business press can sometimes be good sources of information about the backers, the personalities and past effectiveness of those who will become policymakers, and/or which market niche the company is seeking to fill.

The financial stability of an M.C.O. can also be an important piece of information to have. You will want to know if it is sufficiently well financed to weather initial start-up costs and/or a few poorly bid contracts, because the company could well start trying to cut corners if it finds itself in a financial bind. On the other hand, a particularly well-financed M.C.O. may have a sufficient budget to hire excellent marketers and intentionally sign loss-leader contracts in order to position itself in the marketplace. Sometimes, moves such as that can bode well for contracted providers because such expansions usually substantially increase referral flow.

Finally, it can be helpful to peruse the M.C.O.'s advertisements in the benefit management press. If those advertisements exclusively tout cost-containment or low cost, the probability is high that this is not a quality-driven organization. Quality-driven M.C.O.s usually emphasize that fact in their advertisements.

Application Request

From the time you call to request an application, you can begin to notice indicators that will give you information about the quality of the M.C.O. and its attitude toward psychotherapist providers. In nearly all cases, the indicators at this stage should not be utilized as the final criteria with which to determine whether or not to proceed with an application, but they can contribute — sometimes significantly — to your overall picture of the M.C.O. on which a decision should be made about whether or not to become a preferred provider.

One of the things to notice at the time you contact the M.C.O. to request an application is the level of sophistication of the provider relations department staff. If the staff consists of someone with a behavioral health license (licensed marriage and family counsellor, licensed psych nurse, licensed clinical social worker, licensed clinical psychologist or psychiatrist), you can be fairly sure that this M.C.O. is concerned about quality. (As with most generalities, there are a few major exceptions to this.)

However, a licensed behavioral health professional is not an absolute requirement for quality in this position. If you do not find such licensure, you should not conclude that this is a company that is uninterested in quality. I know some nonclinicians who are heads of provider relations departments. They have been in the field for many years now and are very sophisticated. Most experienced E.A.P.s, whether licensed clinicians or not, are in a good position to head the provider relations department. And a few M.C.O.s that cannot afford a licensed professional hire master's level clinicians who do not yet have their license. So it can be helpful to look at the professional qualifications of those who staff provider relations departments for an overall clue to the concern about clinical quality on the part of an M.C.O., but this certainly should not be seen as the primary indicator of quality.

Another early indicator of the quality of an M.C.O. (and its overall concern about collegiality as well as its interest in provider satisfaction) consists of the ease or difficulty of contacting staff members. From your first telephone contact, you should be aware that this experience will probably be indicative of future telephone contacts. Therefore, it will be an indication of the ease or difficulty you will encounter in communications—an all-important area in making a managed care contract work. Do you have to go through an entire menu of options to reach someone? If you leave a message, does it get returned promptly or do you never get a call back and have to leave many subsequent messages? Do you reach a variety of people who do not know how to get you transferred to the right person?

These questions should alert you to some of the potential problems. If you end up playing phone tag (with you calling the provider relations person and that person calling you and both of you continually missing each other), please do not use that experience as necessarily indicative of the quality of the M.C.O. In the past, you have probably experienced phone tag with some of your most effective psychotherapist colleagues, and have found that the problem arises because of busy schedules maintained by effective people rather than because of poor quality.

APPLICATION FORM

The application form is often quite revealing of the managed care company's quality. Probably the clearest indicator of quality on the application form is how the M.C.O. handles specialization verification. As noted previously, M.C.O.s really have only two things to sell to their corporate customers: quality service and low cost. Opinions vary regarding what quality service consists of, but most would agree that a combination of effective and efficient treatment is a primary part of that.

M.C.O.s are doing a great deal of work to define treatment guidelines (see below). But most therapists are aware of the explosion of new knowledge about dynamics and consequent treatment implications in nearly every diagnostic category. This knowledge explosion is such that no treatment generalists can possibly keep up with it on a generalist's level and still be as effective as one who can concentrate upon the new treatment literature while focusing upon only one or two specializations. Consequently, a number of value-based M.C.O.s put substantial effort into differentiating between therapists who have generalist's credentials and those who really specialize. Questions on an application that ask for validation of reported expertise are indicative of an M.C.O. concerned about the quality of its providers.

Patients who belong to ethnic, cultural, sexual orientation, and religious minorities frequently prefer to see a therapist who belongs to the same minority or who is conversant with the special circumstances and issues of members of their minority. Quality-based M.C.O.s are increasingly seeking to cater to those needs. On the other hand, some low cost M.C.O.s are aware that a percentage of their insureds who prefer a therapist of similar minority status will pay privately to someone who will not be reimbursed by the M.C.O. if they cannot find a therapist they like within the M.C.O. When that happens, the M.C.O. saves money because it is not being utilized by one of its insureds. Questions on the application that reflect an aggressive effort to search out minority-sensitive therapists is a sign of a quality-based M.C.O.

CONTRACT ANALYSIS

Probably, the most important decision point regarding whether or not to contract with a managed care organization is when you look at the contract. Try to keep in mind that the contracts constitute binding partnership agreements crafted by the M.C.O.'s attorneys for the purpose of ensuring that the M.C.O. will be well protected financially and legally. Their concern is for the M.C.O.—not for you. While the therapist is usually not seen as an opponent, this is a two-party, legal process document. If there are any inequities in the situation that must be adjudicated in the contract, it is the responsibility of these attorneys to insure that the M.C.O. is not disadvantaged. Thus, the other party—you—will become the disadvantaged participant. For this reason, you should gain as complete an understanding of the contract as possible.

In analyzing both the contract and the provider manual (see the next section), I suggest reading through the material several times. After your initial reading of the provider contract, just sit back and consider how comfortable you would be in working with this M.C.O. from an overall perspective. Think about its structure. Is it a structure that is sensitive to therapist-provider concerns? Overall, does this look like a provider-friendly and consumer-friendly contract? Does it appear to be designed to foster collegial relationships between M.C.O. staff and preferred providers?

After considering your initial reactions, you would do well to inspect the contract extremely carefully. One of the first things to look for is the provider reimbursement rate. As noted previously, reimbursement rate is the one best indicator of the desirability of a managed care company; if the M.C.O. skimps on its reimbursement rate, the chances are high that it will skimp on less obvious areas as well. If it is low or marginal, this will be a clue to look particularly carefully at the rest of the contract. Or it might be a contract breaker—the item that makes the decision for you that this is not a company you wish to contract with.

A related consideration consists of whether or not there is a provider reimbursement rate differential for inpatient services. In most cases, inpatient work costs more for the therapist to deliver than does outpatient work. The absence of an inpatient rate differential may indicate that the M.C.O. has not thought through their preferred providers' needs to the degree they could have.

When reviewing the contract, you should be sure that you truly understand every part of it. If you find a clause you do not understand, stop and try to figure it out. If its meaning remains in any way vague, you should have that clause reviewed by a knowledgeable attorney. A review of the contract in this careful way should alert you to any "problem clauses." Any clauses that are unusual may be problems, and problem clauses should alert you to take another look at the overall contract to ensure that you haven't missed anything.

Sometimes, problem clauses that can be extremely disadvantageous to the therapist are buried deeply in the midst of the contract. In most cases, this is probably not done to take advantage of the therapist. Usually, these clauses simply fall in the middle of the contract because that is where they belong logically in the document. Nevertheless, unless you look carefully, these clauses can remain effectively hidden.

Probably, the most important clause to screen for is the "hold-harmless" clause. There are two kinds of hold-harmless clauses: a one-way hold-harmless and a mutual hold-harmless. Be very careful about signing a one-way hold-harmless because it usually means that if a problem develops, a patient sues and wins, and a judgment is brought, you are considered to be solely responsible regardless of whether the M.C.O. was culpable or not — because you have held the M.C.O. harmless in your contract. Mutual hold-harmless clauses are usually written in such a way that you hold the M.C.O. harmless for anything you do wrong and it holds you harmless for any problems it has engendered. Clearly, this is a preferable contract from the therapist's perspective. But whenever you see the term "hold-harmless" in a contract, it is a good idea to have that contract scrutinized by an attorney.

Another clause to be aware of is the "exclusivity clause." This was frequently incorporated into managed care contracts around 1987 and 1988, but it is now rare. Nevertheless, you should screen for it and decline any contract that carries an exclusivity clause except when it is extremely narrowly defined. Exclusivity clauses specify that if you become a preferred provider for the M.C.O. in this contract, you are prohibited from signing a similar agreement with any other M.C.O.

One potential problem clause may be an unfamiliar reimbursement arrangement. Clauses that require reimbursement arrangements other than fee for service are particularly important to scrutinize for. These might call for case rates, withholds, or some form of capitation. In most cases, capitation and withholds are limited to contracts that involve limited provider groups or independent practice associations (see Chapter 7). Case rates are more frequently found in contracts with preferred provider organizations. Less-familiar reimbursement arrangements can produce effective contracts at times. But the therapist should fully understand them and should ensure that they are written carefully. The author was told by a colleague of a contract she signed which called for her total reimbursement to come from her patients' co-payment. She realized that this was the reimbursement arrangement only AFTER she had already signed the contract. In this case the contract was with an Independent Practice Association (I.P.A.)

If you sign a contract like the one my colleague signed, it is important to terminate it as quickly as possible. Therefore, another important part of the contract consists of the notification time required if you decide to terminate a contract. It is not unusual for an M.C.O. to require a 30-day notice, and I have known of high-quality M.C.O.s requiring 90 days. This is so that they can ensure that current patients are well served, a substitute provider found for that geographic area or specialty, and reports are finalized. It makes sense for an M.C.O. to request a relatively long notification period. But, if you see a notification requirement of 90 days—or especially more than 90 days—be exceptionally careful to examine that contract in minute detail—because you will have to live with it for some time.

A related consideration is the penalty for early termination prior to the completion of the notification period. If it is onerous, that may reflect the M.C.O.'s attitude toward providers.

PROVIDER MANUAL

More of the information you need for making a pro or con decision about signing with a given M.C.O. will come from the provider manual than from any other source. While provider manuals do not exactly carry the reading interest of mystery novels, there are real advantages to familiarizing yourself with them. And if you know what to look for, provider manuals can carry significant suspense and drama.

You will probably find it useful to read through the manual once just to get beginning information and overall impressions. At that time, try to get a sense of who had the major input: clinicians, attorneys, or insurance actuaries. While the input of all of these is probably necessary to complete an appropriate manual, clinical input should be paramount. Certainly clinical compromises suggest possible future problems with this M.C.O.

Often, by examining a manual you can clarify how flexible the M.C.O. is and what its priorities are. Does the manual seem to reflect a flexible, problem-solving approach or a rigid, legalistic, or financial approach? Does it reflect a collegial orientation or a dictatorial one? Do the M.C.O.'s structure and policies make it user-friendly to providers of care? Do you get a sense that the paper flow reporting process suggests a concern with quality and with customer satisfaction, or only with cost control?

After getting that overall picture, there are four important questions you can ask about the M.C.O.'s attitudes which are reflected in the policies outlined by the manual.

Two of these are suggestive of how the M.C.O. views its client patients:

1. What does the manual say about treatment flexibility, particularly the patient's right to continue on a private pay basis if he or she wants

further treatment after that which is authorized by the M.C.O.?

2. What does the provider manual say about treatment decision appeals?

Answers to the other two questions are suggestive of how the M.C.O. views its psychotherapist providers:

1. What is the policy about provider reimbursement for missed appointments?
2. Do you get a sense that the time demands required to implement the paper flow reporting process will leave you a satisfactory per-hour reimbursement rate?

Treatment Flexibility

The first of these four questions, treatment flexibility, is extremely important to most-appropriate patient care. It reflects a willingness to spend the cost to get knowledgeable case managers and to give them the flexibility to substitute one part of the benefit for another on the client's behalf (within the scope of each contract). For example, in the past, employers often purchased extensive inpatient benefits while skimping on outpatient benefits. Sometimes, intensive outpatient care is an appropriate step to try prior to resorting to inpatient care. Benefit treatment flexibility provisions can allow the case manager to trade inpatient days for outpatient visits (usually on a one day for two visit basis) Such flexibility provisions should be written into corporate benefit contracts whenever possible. However, that becomes more difficult if the manual simply disallows it. Such a disallowance may reflect a corporate bias against benefit flexibility.

Another aspect of the flexibility issue consists of what happens after the authorized visits are completed. Increasingly, employers request contracts that allow only for five to six visits. These are usually called "Crisis Intervention Only" contracts. If an employee of one of those employers requests more visits, it is disallowed by his benefit package — not necessarily by the treatment manual. When that occurs, patients sometimes want to extend their visits and are willing to pay out-of-pocket for this possibility.

Some M.C.O.s disallow such an out-of-pocket continuation of care, based upon implied promises to the employer of no (or little) out-of-pocket expense to employees or based upon a fear that therapist providers will use this process as a private-client-generating mechanism. When M.C.O.s find ways through such objections in order to insure continuity of care for patients, they demonstrate an attitude of caring about the insured patients, even when their competitive position requires them to write restrictive benefit contracts.

Treatment Decision Appeals

The second question, which is reflective of the M.C.O.'s attitude toward its policyholder patients, has to do with treatment decision appeals. What does the manual say regarding disputes between the patient (or the patient and therapist) and the case manager regarding appropriate care? Is there an appeals process? If so, do you sense that this M.C.O. sees appeals as disruptive or as something to respond to in a constructive, collegial manner? Is the appeals process one you feel that you can live with? If the appeal can be made only to the case manager's direct supervisor with no provider input, you may feel uncomfortable regarding this contract. Or if the manual has any clause that suggests you may be penalized in your provider profile should you appeal on behalf of your patient, you should feel some discomfort regarding signing this contract. (The author has filed appeals twice—with different managed care companies—and as nearly as I can tell there was no provider profile penalty in either case. Both resulted in modifications on the part of the case managers but did not give my clients all that we were asking for. Both case managers have continued to work with me cooperatively and collegially. In another case, American Psych-Management, an appeal was initiated automatically for me and, even though it was ultimately denied, they took pains to help work out an alternative care arrangement for my client.)

If the manual calls for a series of possible appeal steps with provider input at several levels, you can assume that a fairly careful hearing will be possible. Good M.C.O.s usually are as concerned with getting the most effective treatment as they are with cost containment, and they usually hire case managers who are more concerned about patients receiving quality care than about proving themselves right.

Missed Appointments

The company's policy regarding patients who fail to keep appointments is a good quick indicator of the M.C.O.'s overall attitude regarding a concern for provider satisfaction. Policies among M.C.O.s differ substantially on this issue. A few allow providers to charge for at least some reimbursement at any time a client fails to keep an appointment. Usually, the client is to be billed under these policies, but occasionally the M.C.O. agrees to make the reimbursement itself—especially if the failed appointment was an initial appointment. Other M.C.O.s allow for at least a partial reimbursement under some circumstances and not when other circumstances prevail. Many M.C.O.s simply prohibit any billing from the therapist under any circumstances for appointments that have not been kept by the client.

Paperwork Time

Paperwork time is the second issue covered in the manual that can give you an indication of the M.C.O.'s attitudes toward its psychotherapist providers. Since therapists have often reduced their rates in order to work with M.C.O.s, and since we get paid on the basis of our time, the per-hour real reimbursement rate is critical. M.C.O.s with complicated or lengthy paperwork or telephone reporting procedures increase the cost of doing business for their therapists—sometimes prohibitively. Your real per-hour reimbursement is a function of clinical time plus paperwork and telephone reporting time divided by the number of reimbursable clinical sessions. You should always average out your real reimbursable rates for a number of patients before deciding whether or not a given M.C.O. is reimbursing you at the rate you wish. Some understanding of the paperwork drag on real reimbursement rates can be obtained from your reading of the manual, but often you will have to wait until you have actually experienced implementing the contract for awhile before you will be in a position to really determine this.

Notification of Benefits and Changes

What is the M.C.O.'s policy regarding notifying providers of benefits and benefit changes? Some M.C.O.s do this through periodically sending updates on all of their contracts with employers. Others try to personalize this information by providing therapists with a careful understanding of the client's current benefit structure (including copayment schedules) at the time of the initial referral of each client. A few M.C.O.s use both procedures. Of course, when a managed care company utilizes both procedures, that is an indication that it is concerned about making the process user-friendly for the therapist and reducing mistakes for the sake of the patient.

However, my own experience is that the individual notification at the time of each referral is critical. Those M.C.O.s relying exclusively on periodic updates of M.C.O.-employer contract changes in benefit structure are utilizing a procedure that is complicated, time-consuming (which means expensive for the therapist), and filled with potential problems. It means that the therapist must hope he gets all updates and none get lost in the mail. He must then change them in his files — usually on a once-per-month-per-company basis. That file must then be referred to whenever a new client comes in.

If you see this kind of process listed as the sole option for determining current benefit status, you should probably factor in at the beginning a per-client expense equal to at least one-half hour of your therapy time plus an additional expense of one to two hours for anticipated costs due to reimbursement losses attached to professional fees that have become non-collectable due to benefit change information that has not been clarified until after services have already been performed.

Claims Processing Procedures

You should also check out the claims processing procedures of the M.C.O. Some M.C.O.s sign agreements with other insurance companies to do all of the work except claims processing. When that occurs, the resulting "pass-through" claims procedure requires that you send your claims into the M.C.O., which reviews them and then passes them on to the insurance company. Of course, this extra step complicates and delays the claims processing. The problem is compounded to the point that it is sometimes nearly unworkable when the M.C.O. disclaims any responsibility for the ultimate claim payment. This is, of course, within the right of the M.C.O., since — by contract — it is not the ultimate payor. However, some managed care companies with this type of contract do accept responsibility for ironing out any difficulties.

IMPLEMENTATION

In many cases, you will not truly be able to determine whether or not a given managed care affiliation will work out for you until you begin implementing the contract, after you have begun to see clients referred from that M.C.O. Very quickly, you will get a sense of the time demands. You should try to get a familiarity with the forms and do a few cases before deciding the impact of the time demands in order to eliminate the bias of time spent solely because of unfamiliarity with the procedures.

After a few client cases have been processed, however, it is a good idea to start keeping records of your paperwork and telephone time for each client so that you can figure out the true time spent per clinical hour. Once you have that information, you can divide your full time (clinical and paperwork) into the reimbursement rate to get your true per-minute reimbursement rate. Then multiply this figure by 60 to get your true per-hour reimbursement rate. Average this true reimbursement rate over several cases to get an idea of your average per-hour reimbursement for this M.C.O. If it is too low, you need to do something: drop your contract, see patients from this M.C.O. only when you have otherwise free time, or stay only on an inactive status with this company.

When making this decision, consider the sophistication of the case managers you end up working with. If the true reimbursement rate is acceptable but marginal, you might still decide to become inactive or drop this contract if the case managers are unsophisticated. This is because sooner or later you may very likely end up spending a great deal of time educating them or fixing problems which would not have occurred if they had seen the issues/dynamics more clearly. When problems occur, they will be resolved more efficiently if the provider relations department is truly empowered to help therapists negotiate the system on behalf of their patients. So the collegiality, willingness, and power to help therapists negotiate the system on behalf of their patients will be a strong indicator of whether or not problems down the road could turn into a time and energy trap for you.

Once you are working as a preferred provider, you can clarify whether or not there is a provider advisory panel. If there is one, it is a sign that the M.C.O. is concerned about its providers and tries to listen to them. That, in turn, suggests that problems down the road can get resolved quickly and efficiently. If there is a provider advisory panel, I suggest that you volunteer for a position on it.

SUMMARY OF
CHOICE INDICATORS
FOR EVALUATING MANAGED CARE COMPANIES

A. Investigation phase:

1. What is the reputation of the M.C.O. among local employee assistance professionals?
2. What is the reputation of this M.C.O. among your local colleagues and in your state professional organization?
3. Check behavioral health care newsletters such as *Open Minds* for their comments about this M.C.O.
4. Check business newspapers or the company's stock prospectus for information about the company's financial stability.
5. Check out this M.C.O.'s advertising in the benefit management press. Those advertisements are intended to make the M.C.O. appealing to benefit managers. Does this M.C.O. appeal to you as well?

B. Application Request:

6. What is the level of sophistication of the provider relations department staff?
7. Does the M.C.O. appear to make it easy or difficult for providers to access staff members?

C. Application Form:

8. Does the application ask for some kind of verification of specialty training?
9. Does it ask about multicultural sensitivity or membership in a cultural or ethnic minority?

D. Contract Analysis:

10. Overall, does this look like a provider-friendly contract?
11. Does this contract appear to be designed to foster collegial relationships between M.C.O. staff and preferred providers?
12. Is the provider reimbursement rate an acceptable one for your profession?
13. Is there a reimbursement rate differential for inpatient treatment?

14. Does the contract have hidden clauses that can be damaging to the therapist-provider?
15. Does it have a hold-harmless clause? If it does, is the clause one-way or mutual?
16. Does it have an exclusivity clause?
17. Does it provide for a fee-for-service reimbursement arrangement or is some unfamiliar reimbursement arrangement utilized?
18. How long does it take to cancel the contract?
19. Are there any penalties to the provider if he/she cancels the contract?

E. Provider Manual:

20. Overall, are the policies written into the manual ones you can live with ethically, legally, and functionally?
21. Do you get a sense that the manual was written by legal experts or by clinicians?
22. Is there an emphasis on collegiality in problem-solving?
23. Does this M.C.O.'s structure make it user-friendly to the providers of care?
24. Does the company's paper flow reporting process suggest a concern with quality, customer satisfaction, or only cost control?
25. What kind of benefit flexibility does the manual suggest is possible?
26. What is this M.C.O.'s policy regarding clients who wish to go private pay after their visit authorizations end?
27. Is there an appeals process? If so, is it one you can live with?
28. Do you get a sense that this M.C.O. sees appeals as disruptive or does it respond to them in a constructive, collegial manner?
29. What is the company's no-show policy?
30. Do you get a sense that the time demands required to implement the paper flow reporting process leave you a satisfactory per-hour reimbursement rate?
31. What is the company's policy regarding notification of benefit changes? Is this done through generic mailings or is there an effort made for individual notification on an as-needed basis?
32. What are the claims policies of this M.C.O.? If they do pass-through claims processing, do they accept responsibility for that?

F. Implementation:

33. Do the time demands required to implement the paper flow reporting process leave you a satisfactory per-hour reimbursement rate?

34. What is the average amount of telephone time required for managed care processing for each patient with this company?
35. For each of your cases, you should try to add the paper flow reporting time and the telephone time required for processing the case to the clinical time and then divide them into the permissible billable hours (usually this consists of total clinical hours). Does this net real per-hour income yield you a sufficient hourly income?
36. What is the sophistication of the case managers you end up working with?
37. Do the M.C.O.'s staff members work with you cooperatively and collegially when there are problems?
38. Is the provider relations department truly capable and empowered to help therapists negotiate the system on behalf of their patients?
39. Is there a provider advisory panel for the managed care company? If one exists, does it have the ear of executives who are able to have an impact on policy?

NOTES

1. Quoted by Monica Oss at the Fifth Annual National Managed Health Care Congress on 04/13/93. Figures derived from in-house survey by "Open Minds."
2. Quote taken by permission from private communication (letter) from Maureen Cardiff, M.S.W., B.C.D. to Ian Shaffer, M.D., vice-president of medical affairs and chief medical officer, American PsychManagement, Inc., on 3/30/93.

7/
Future Marketing:
Near-Term Repositioning

Even as you seek to position yourself in today's marketplace by providing a high quality of service and carefully choosing your managed care partners it makes sense to look to the future. There are three reasons for this:

1. Most marketing efforts take one to two years to produce good results.
2. Behavioral health care financing in general and managed care in particular are tied to corporate employer-M.C.O. contracts, which are transitory, usually lasting only one to three years. The time limits on these contracts can result in sudden reductions in the flow of referrals for any therapist who is on the receiving end of that referral pipeline. A substantial referral reduction can occur when most (or even a significant percentage) of the patients sent to you from any particular M.C.O. come from only one local employer. This entire employee group can then be prohibited from seeing you if the M.C.O.-corporate contract expires and the employer signs with a different managed care organization that does not include you as a preferred provider.
3. Probably the most important reason to market on a time-line basis for the near-term future is that the structure of behavioral health care delivery systems—especially managed care organizations—is changing rapidly. This structural change will result in some therapists positioning themselves for large, somewhat specialized flows of referrals and other therapists getting increasingly left with very few or no referrals.

Thus, understanding the near-term future of managed care is critical to any therapist who wishes to position himself or herself for successful marketing in that future marketplace. Predictions are always filled with possibilities for error. But there are three techniques we can utilize to turn prediction into probability forecasting in order to understand the probable near-term future of this industry: (1) looking at the medical managed care model, which has become a forerunner for many of the trends in behavioral managed care, (2) utilizing the current predictions of those whose past predictions have turned out to be correct in this industry, and (3) considering the trends anticipated by trendsetters — those who are in a position to initiate, to implement, or to track those trends.

In this chapter, the comments of people drawn from, or familiar with, each of those categories will be discussed. All three of the predictors indicate relatively similar scenarios for the near future in behavioral managed care. Such consistency lends verification and adds verisimilitude to the predictions, even though absolute proof must await the future. These predictions suggest changes that will affect the structure, process, financing, and independence of today's clinicians' practices.

Although M.C.O.s fit into the purview of the recently formed Utilization Review Accreditation Commission (U.R.A.C.), which has established national operating standards, acceptance of those standards and submission to U.R.A.C. for accreditation are voluntary. So far, most managed care companies have declined to participate in U.R.A.C. Given this absence so far of either accepted standards or an accrediting body that is utilized, many observers expect the behavioral managed care field to come under increasing governmental regulation. In fact, the Clinton administration will undoubtedly institute substantial regulation in the very near future, thus ensuring a three-part power structure underlying managed care: corporate benefits departments, insurance companies, and the federal government.

At the time of writing this book, the American Health Security Act proposals are still tentative, and the degree to which they will be modified before being enacted are still not clear. But they will be built upon a managed care foundation. Even after modifications from Congress, their impact will be so strong that all therapists will need to position themselves quickly for this change. This will be discussed in greater length in Chapter 8.

In the meantime, an extremely dynamic marketplace exists with considerable consolidation, fractioning, and creation of niches by M.C.O.s. Of those three changes, consolidation is especially apparent in the "insurancization" of behavioral managed care, as major insurance companies purchase large managed fee-for-service behavioral health companies. We have already seen Ætna Life and Casualty purchase Human Affairs International, Inc.; M.C.C. Co., Inc. become a subsidiary of CIGNA; and LifeLink become a subsidiary of PacifiCare Health Systems as well as affiliating with Columbia General Life Insurance.

NEAR-TERM CHANGES AHEAD

As we discussed in Chapter 5, M.C.O.s are seeking to find and fill market niches. Whereas in the first few years of active managed behavioral health care the competition among M.C.O.s was almost exclusively based upon cost containment, value (a combination of quality and price) is now beginning to be emphasized as a market niche. So a spectrum is emerging which reaches from M.C.O.s that focus exclusively upon low cost on one end to those that emphasize value (quality plus cost containment) on the other end, with most M.C.O.s falling somewhere between these two groups.

Most of the near-term changes that will occur in the behavioral health care industry derive from one of the above two imperatives: cost reduction or quality enhancement. But their implementation varies according to where along the low cost–high value continuum a particular M.C.O. falls. These changes, which can be expected to solidify in the next few years, include:

1. Alternatives to inpatient hospitalization,
2. Subcontracting with psychotherapist provider groups, leading to a concomitant reduction in solo practices,
3. Risk sharing and risk shifting,
4. Reduction of in-house utilization review by M.C.O.s,
5. Total Quality Management, including extensive outcomes measurement,
6. Preferred guidelines for diagnostic-specific treatment,
7. Computerization at every level, including individual providers.

1. Alternatives to Inpatient Hospitalization

Since inpatient hospitalization is seen as a particularly expensive treatment modality, cost sensitivity has driven M.C.O.s to develop alternatives to inpatient treatment. Two of those alternatives consist of development of intensive outpatient protocols and partial hospitalization. Both of those alternatives have been predicted for some time, with relatively little utilization so far.[1] However, their utilization should increase substantially in the near future as better mechanisms are put into place for implementing them. Behavioral health hospitals themselves are quickly developing this range of services. Some hospital chains are developing their own preferred provider organization that will be marketed directly to employers. In the process of these initiatives, hospitals and hospital chains are developing preferred relationships with specific local therapists who can benefit by mutual referrals.

2. Provider Group Subcontracting

As we discussed in Chapter 3, a very strong trend in the managed behavioral health care industry is subcontracting to groups of psychotherapists. This is a procedure that has worked very well for M.C.O.s in the medical health care field, where it gained widespread use in a brief period of time. The intensity and speed of this trend toward group contracting in the behavioral health care field is presently so strong that solo practitioners may find themselves in the next few years having a sense of déjà vu. In the last few years, therapists without managed care contracts found substantial parts of their client flow diverted to therapists who held such contracts.

Similarly, solo practitioners may soon find increasing segments of their preferred provider managed care client flow diverted to therapists who are members of group practices. In fact, in an article for "The California Therapist," Mary Riemersma and Richard Leslie, the executive director and legal counsel for the California Association of Marriage and Family Therapists, conclude ". . . if one is interested in participating in managed care in the future, and one wants to assure himself/herself a greater role with managed care, the group practice model is preferred."[2] In the next couple of years, we will probably see a large number of provider groups contracting with M.C.O.s. Most of these will probably be multidisciplinary coalitions.

3. Risk Sharing and Risk Shifting

One of the fastest growing and most pervasive changes in the behavioral health care delivery industry at this time is risk shifting. In the last few years, the cost containment benefits from managed care (both H.M.O.s and P.P.O.s) have been disappointing. According to the Employee Benefits Research Institute, "the costs of such plans have been rising more than 13% a year. . . ."[3] Moreover, some M.C.O.s have submitted inappropriately low bids for business and have then had apparent difficulty in meeting operating expenses. Thus, from the perspective of M.C.O.s it makes sense to shift at least some of the burden of cost estimating (i.e., financial risk) and cost absorption onto psychotherapist providers. M.C.O.s can sub-contract to provider groups for significant portions of the functions necessary to service their contract with employers. If they wish, M.C.O.s can get out from under their own financial risks by simply shifting their risks to subcontracted psychotherapist providers through group contracts.

When taken to its limits, this process can make it possible for a managed care company to position itself with little more financial risk exposure than that of a broker. The process is accomplished by the taking of large blocs of potential clients who were previously referred to individual clinicians on a direct-payment basis and referring them instead to groups of therapists who agree to at-risk or risk-sharing contracts.

There are many mechanisms which a M.C.O. can use to share risk with providers, but the most common is capitation. Capitation consists of paying a certain amount to therapist groups for treatment of blocs of employees or insureds regardless of the number who may utilize treatment and regardless of the length or intensity of treatment. The payment is usually determined by a process in which groups of therapists submit competing bids for a contract to treat a bloc of employees or insureds. The therapist group that submits the lowest bid usually wins the contract as long as all of the other requirements of the M.C.O. are met as well. And the bids are based upon charging a certain monthly amount per covered employee or insured. This per capita basis of fee structuring is why it is called capitation.

A good explanation of how this works and what therapists should be aware of is summarized by "Psychotherapy Finances" newsletter. They note that (with capitated fees) "there is considerable risk involved for the provider, especially if the volume of clients and the services required exceed expectations. . . . At-risk fees will vary, depending on the type of contract, the level of services provided, and the local competition. There is, however, some basic information that providers must have before bidding on a capitated contract. For instance, many companies will try to give you vague figures when reporting on their recent utilization experience (percentage of employees who actually utilize therapy services). But you need good data to estimate the number of people who are likely to ask for treatment, as well as the type and length of treatment."[4]

Another piece which needs to be factored into the bid is the overhead of administering the contract. "A reasonable administrative overhead for a group practice is about 20%," notes Alan Axelson, president and medical director for InterCare Psychiatric Services. Axelson says "The cost is swelling as group practices add specialized support staff—sometimes with the sole responsibility of interpreting outpatient benefits for clients."[5]

In addition to the per diem capitation mechanisms noted here, there are other methods for sharing risk. One of these is case fee reimbursement. This usually applies to assessments and means that the therapist is reimbursed at a set rate whether the assessment consists of one, two, or three sessions.[6] Ms. Tamara Cagney is a leading consultant in the E.A.P. and managed care fields. In an article that provides a good overall explanation of current behavioral health care risk shifting,[7] she notes, "Current provider reimbursement arrangements are subject to revision as computer technologies allow for more detailed tracking of utilization and comparison with standard treatment protocols. Use of withholds, incentives and risk sharing will be combined in new ways with fee-for-service, per diem, discount and case fee reimbursement methodologies."[7]

4. Reduction of In-House Utilization Review by M.C.O.s

The primary function of early attempts at managing behavioral health care was utilization review. This was seen as particularly important because of a relatively small but significant number of hospitals that operated inappropriately in a variety of areas—primarily admissions and duration of treatment. The excesses of even this relatively small group of hospitals resulted in such high expenditures that utilization programs brought large savings. Thus, utilization review very quickly became a cornerstone of cost containment through its twin functions of evaluating both quality and necessity of treatment.

Although utilization review (U.R.) began as somewhat infrequent concurrent or even retrospective review of inpatient programs, soon the concept was applied to most outpatient behavioral health programs. It was also expanded to include preauthorization. Under this arrangement payment will not be made for any treatment which has not been preauthorized. And preauthorization will not be given unless there is a review of the prospective treatment plan and its rationale. As U.R. has become more pervasive, implementation costs have skyrocketed while the improvement in cost containment has been limited. Therefore, a shift is now taking place to more quality-based mechanisms, especially Total Quality Management (T.Q.M.) for insuring quality as well as true cost containment. These are increasingly being supplemented by retrospective utilization review, often accompanied by retrospective fines and payments.

5. Total Quality Management

As with a wide spectrum of other segments of American industry, many of the larger preferred provider behavioral health care organizations (value-based M.C.O.s) are moving heavily and rapidly into T.Q.M. (Total Quality Management). This is understandable. Jerry Bowles, author of "Beyond Quality," and many other management consultants note that "In this age of tough competition TQM is the minimum requirement for staying in the game."[8] Total quality management is a process for:

1. Investigating bottlenecks or effectiveness problems through a disparate team (which is usually drawn from management, line staff, consumer, and possibly other groups),
2. Analyzing procedures to ensure that they are as effective as possible, and
3. Comparing a company's procedures with those of the most effective company they can find (even if it is in a different industry) in a process known as "benchmarking."

T.Q.M. consultants suggest focusing on only one or two areas initially. That is what behavioral health companies are doing. For example, American PsychManagement has primarily worked on developing fast, problem-free claims processing. But most of the value-based M.C.O.s have emphasized treatment efficiency or treatment effectiveness, or both, through a process called "Outcomes Research."

One can measure treatment efficiency by reviewing cases to determine the length of treatment time necessary to effect various changes. Changes may be defined functionally or symptomatically. Functional change can be measured by comparing DSM-IV Global Assessment of Functioning

(G.A.F.) Scales at the beginning and end of treatment. Symptom changes can be measured by comparing presenting symptoms with the number and intensity of symptoms at the time of discharge.

Treatment effectiveness can be measured through satisfaction surveys and longitudinal research. Satisfaction surveys consist of brief checkoff or sentence completion sheets that are generally sent to patients soon after completion of treatment. They are utilized by nearly every major preferred provider M.C.O. Longitudinal research generally focuses more on long-term effectiveness by looking at such criteria as one- and five-year follow-up study results, recidivism rates, and analysis of the patient's subsequent medical usage (called medical offset studies).

As data accumulate, it will be possible to compare average treatment efficiency and effectiveness of any one therapist against the averages for other therapists for any given diagnosis. More important, it will be increasingly possible to compare different treatment methods for efficiency and effectiveness. Some hospitals and some methodologies will stand out. The valuable ones are labeled "benchmarks" and the ineffective ones are labeled "outliers." The benchmark therapists will then be used as models. Benchmark methodologies will increasingly be studied to develop preferred treatment approaches for each diagnosis.

6. Preferred Guidelines for Diagnostic-Specific Treatment

One of the most important tenants of the total quality management movement is product or service consistency. In other fields, mechanisms that insure that every nut or bolt has the same amount of steel in it or that every hamburger patty has the same percentage of fat content pay off in the long run because they insure quality in the finished product. At first, it may seem that service consistency would be impossible in the field of behavioral health care. But a mechanism for getting closer to that goal consists of treatment data comparisons by diagnosis which illuminate more effective and less effective treatment approaches. And M.C.O.s are expecting that over time these comparisons can result in preferred treatment guidelines that are grounded in statistically validated clinical studies. The rationale for this was explained well by Ms. Tamara Cagney, a consultant on employee assistance programs and managed care, when she said, "When strong scientific agreement exists regarding proper care. . . relatively little variation occurs in treatment patterns. . . ."[9]

Most of the M.C.O.s that are accumulating data about treatment approaches are linking that data specifically to diagnoses. Thus far, it appears that they are seeking to be as inclusive as possible of all of the DSM diagnoses except for V codes. This means that eventually each value-based M.C.O. will develop preferred treatment guidelines for each diagnoses.

Some M.C.O.s are not waiting for statistically validated treatment guidelines, but are seeking intermediate routes to what they conclude is the most appropriate care. An example is M.C.C. Managed Behavioral Care, Inc. In their December, 1992 newsletter, John Bartlett, M.D., the corporate medical director, was quoted as follows: "I am a manager who is charged with coming up with a sound approach to what appropriate care is, and that's what we're trying to accomplish here. Practice guidelines are a part of that, but only in that they need to be looked at and continuously improved. Right now we improve the standards through an interactive consensus process; down the road we're building in some scientific approaches to measure outcomes and then using that information to revise the standards in more valid, reliable ways."

Dr. Bartlett goes on to present a good understanding of why managed care companies are engaging in this effort. He notes, "One of the major problems in this area is that there are no accepted standards of care. The practice guidelines combined with outcomes research will benefit providers in the future both by contributing to the greater policy discussions about what is appropriate, and by providing the data that will advance the state of the art. The real opportunity here may be to expand mental health and substance abuse coverage for people, because we'll be able to prove that it accomplishes something. . . showing that making people less depressed actually decreases their medical costs, increases their productivity, and decreases their absenteeism. Proving results will make it easier for corporations to continue funding mental health and substance abuse care because the results will justify the investment."[10]

7. Computerization at Every Level

As one can imagine from the goals and methods of T.Q.M., as well as for such efforts as establishing diagnostic-specific preferred treatment guidelines, the amount of data necessary to implement these goals and methods is enormous. For example, M.C.C. Managed Behavioral Care has set up an outcomes evaluation module in cooperation with the University of Minnesota just to track and record various treatment decisions as a part of the ongoing process of development and modification of their treatment standards.

Of course, all of the raw data comes from providers and case managers. As noted in Chapter 6, psychotherapist providers are already burdened with large paperwork tasks for managed care. Increasingly, computerization will be seen as one of the very few ways to accomplish those tasks within a sufficiently acceptable time frame to leave overall per-hour reimbursement rates at a reasonable level.

Both insurance companies and managed care organizations will increasingly insist upon computerization. Depending upon whom one speaks to, the cost of processing paperwork in the overall health care industry has been estimated between $40 billion and $90 billion dollars a year![11] Richard Landen, spokesman for the Health Insurance Association of America, states that, "The first step in slashing processing costs. . . is developing standard *electronic* forms." He notes that, "Several standards for electronic forms, including patient bills have been approved by the American National Standards Institute, the federally sanctioned body that handles such matters." Electronic transfers of money—from an insurer to a hospital, for example—is another goal.[12] "The workgroup for Electronic Data Interchange, a health care industry coalition formed at government request, has called for major insurers and hospitals to have the ability to communicate electronically by the end of 1994."[13]

This chapter reflects only a part of the health care industry. We have focused here primarily upon two of the three primary forces driving change in the industry: insurance and managed care preferred provider organizations. A third powerful force consists of change initiated by the federal government. In the next chapter, we will discuss the new federal initiative: the American Health Security Act.

NOTES

1. Monica E. Oss and John Krizay, Behavioral Health Industry Statistics Monograph 42. *"Industry Statistics: Partial Hospitalization's Time Has Yet to Come: Only Small Portion of Market Share."* Open Minds Publication 1992 Published by Behavioral Health Industry News, Inc., Gettysburg, Pa. 1992.
2. Mary Riemersma and Richard Leslie, in article *"Managed Care in the '90s, A Continuing Evolution"* in *"The California Therapist,"* November/December, 1992 issue, Page 15.
3. *Los Angeles Times* Newspaper. 8-30-92. Page 1 in Section D (Business section).
4. *"Psychotherapy Finances"* Newsletter Volume 18, #11, Issue 223. Page 3.
5. *"Psychotherapy Finances"* Newsletter Volume 18, #10, Issue 222.
6. Cagney, Tamara, in article *"Risk Shifting and Managed Care, Should EAPs be Concerned?"* *"Employee Assistance"* magazine. Vol. 4, #7, February, 1992. Page 26.
7. Cagney, Tamara. *"Risk Shifting and Managed Care, Should EAPs be Concerned?"* in *"Employee Assistance"* magazine, Vol. 4, #7, February, 1992. Page 28.
8. Mathews, Jay and Katel, Peter: article *"The Cost of Quality"* in *Newsweek* Magazine, September 7, 1992, page 49.
9. Cagney, Tamara. From article *"Risk Shifting and Managed Care"* in *Employee Assistance* magazine. Vol. 4, #7. February, 1992. Page 34.
10. Bartlett, John, M.D. in article *"New Clinical Standards Available to Providers"* in *"The Provider"* a newsletter sent to its preferred providers by M.C.C. Behavioral Care. December, 1992 edition. Page 1.
11. Mariann Caprino for Associated Press in *Los Angeles Daily News* Newspaper, 1-15-93. Business section page 1.
12. Ibid.
13. Ibid.

8/
The Impact of the American Health Security Act

As this book goes to press, the outlines of the next revolution in behavioral health care delivery are beginning to emerge. These outlines constitute the framework of the American Health Security Act: a national health care initiative so firmly built upon managed care that it was originally entitled "managed competition." Because managed care is the underlying framework for the American Health Security Act, we can expect that in the near future there will be even more incentive for psychotherapists to become affiliated with managed care organizations.

The health security initiative has many purposes. One of them is to contain health care costs—including behavioral health care costs. Another goal is to extend health care to the 33 million Americans who are currently uninsured.

On March 29, 1993 the first public meeting of the White House Task Force on Health Care Reform was chaired by Vice President Al Gore. In it, he pledged that the administration's plan will, ". . . guarantee health security for every American, bring down the rising costs of health care that threaten each of us, maintain the quality of care and people's right to choose their doctors and simplify the system and cut through the paperwork."[1]

The proposals anticipate accomplishing these goals primarily through a model like that shown in Figure 4 and further detailed below.[2]

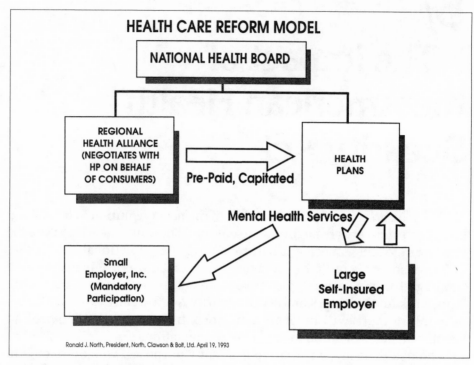

Figure 4: Health Care Reform Model

1. A National Health Board (N.H.B.) will set policy and probably set caps on provider fees, hospital fees, and/or insurance premiums.

2. The National Health Board will set up Regional Health Alliances (R.H.A.s), which will be in charge of implementing N.H.B. policies. Most R.H.A.s will be statewide, with a separate R.H.A. for each state. However, some states, such as Texas, California, New York, and possibly Alaska, may have two or even three R.H.A.s. States such as Hawaii and Oregon which have already instituted health care reform will probably be allowed to utilize their in-place reforms as the basis for their statewide R.H.A.s as long as the state R.H.A.s meet the National Health Board's minimal guidelines.

3. The National Health Board will administer universal employer-sponsored health care coverage, probably through a requirement that all employers sponsor every worker's health insurance. Medical and behavioral health care plans presently retained by "small" employers will be replaced. The definition of "small" will probably become a

issue, and may be one of the last issues to be decided. It could be set anywhere between 100 employees and 500 employees; if set low enough, it could encompass up to 80% of the nation's employees. The employees will be folded into the Regional Health Alliances, set up by the National Health Board, which will act as massive health-purchasing cooperatives. "Large" employers must offer similar coverage. They will be able to do this through joining a Regional Health Alliance or by contracting through their own corporate alliance, as long as the insurance obtained meets the requirements set by the National Health Board.

4. Each Regional Health Alliance will contract with providers through regional managed care companies called Health Plans (H.P.s). H.P.s will be composed of H.M.O.s, P.P.O.s, and — most likely — coalitions of Health Maintenance Organizations, Independent Practice Associations, H.P.G.s (Hospital-Provider Groups), G.W.W.s (Groups Without Walls), and any other permutation of managed care which can offer a competitive package. Some Regional Health Alliances can be expected to contract with only four to six health plans and others may contract with a multitude of them.

   There will probably be a mandate for at least a minimum Health Maintenance Organization presence. Therefore, Regional Health Alliances that contract with only four to six H.P.s will restrict the number of possible participating companies considerably. This indicates that the H.P.s in those states will be huge cooperatives composed of a variety of managed care companies and groups, and that any therapist who is not connected to one of those will be limited in his ability to attract new patients.

The Regional Health Alliances will pool together all employees of "small" businesses in the region, everyone in the region who is presently uninsured, and probably everyone who is now enrolled in a medicaid or medicare program. Thus, they will represent very large numbers of consumers. This enormous size should enable the R.H.A.s to negotiate very favorable insurance rates or alternative pricing arrangements. When they contract with Health Plans, we can expect bidding wars, with the ultimate contracts going to the H.P.s that offer the most attractive package of low price, inclusive coverage of all elements in the basic health plan, and possibly quality of care. As noted above, most H.P.s will probably be composed of coalitions of existing managed care structures that will continue to subcontract with psychotherapist providers for delivery of care. Theoretically, the H.P. coalitions will utilize their size to exert economic clout, enabling them to obtain high quality service from providers at low prices.

Employees who want more than the basic plan will have the option of adding elements through a supplemental insurance policy. "Large" employers can opt for any health care plan as long as it meets the basic requirements set by the National Health Board. However, there will be pressure—possibly in the form of taxes on "excessive" coverage beyond a basic core plan—to contain costs.

It is anticipated that these mechanisms will be supplemented by the following implementing proposals:

Short-term price controls on providers of care.

A lid on the cost of insurance premiums.

A cut in insurance red tape (probably starting with forms standardization).

Coverage for long-term care. The starting date for this will probably be delayed because of the huge costs of coverage for long-term care.

Greater roles for non-physician providers (particularly physician-assistants and nurses).

Coverage expansion. The reform is being designed "with the special needs of the undeserved very much in mind."[3]

An emphasis on services that are home- and community-based.

An emphasis on preventive medicine.

Coverage for preexisting medical conditions (through barring insurers from refusing to cover people with preexisting medical conditions).

Equality with physical ailments for coverage of mental disorders and drug abuse.[4] This will not be fully implemented until 2001.

These changes carry many implications for psychotherapists:

1. Since the American Health Security Act is based upon the managed care framework, it is even more imperative that psychotherapists familiarize themselves with managed care and affiliate with it in its various forms.

2. Capitation may become extremely attractive as a payment mechanism that can preserve income in a system that limits fee-for-service payments.

3. Affiliation with providers' groups will become an even stronger imperative for therapists. This will be a requirement for those who wish to contract on a capitated basis.

4. Both price controls and, particularly, the lid on insurance premiums will mean that an even greater emphasis will be placed upon cost containment. Any therapist who can provide greater cost efficiency without compromise of quality will increase his or her marketability.

5. An even closer coordination between primary care physicians and mental health professionals will occur because of the increased cost containment pressures. Based on an evaluation of data generated by the Federal Employees Health Benefits Administration Arthur L. Kovacs, Ph.D., a special consultant to the committee for the Advancement of Professional Practice of the American Psychological Association, has noted that ". . .70% of all insurance billing for individual psychotherapy is rendered by non-psychiatric physicians. . . ."[5]

    Capitated physician groups have begun to subcontract with multispecialty behavioral health groups for psychotherapy, enabling them to benefit from psychotherapists' lower costs and more specific behavioral health training. This trend should accelerate after implementation of the American Health Security Act.

6. The eventual equality of coverage for behavioral health care with medical health care has a number of potential implications. If there is the perception of more liberal funding for behavioral health care than for medical health care, events that occurred in the mid 1980s may reoccur. When federally sponsored medical care payment guidelines based on diagnostic-related groups began to restrict the profitability of general medical hospitals, many in the medical establishment invested in freestanding psychiatric hospitals, which were free of those restrictions. The resulting drive for profits led to marketing abuses. And the wide profit margins were a major factor in the behavioral health care cost explosion. The extension of managed care into behavioral health was largely for the purpose of containing this cost increase.

    The reader would be wise to be alert to such a potential profit differential because the resulting massive investments can be expected to profoundly distort whatever phase of behavioral health care it touches.

7. A wide range of newly viable specialties and market niches should emerge. These will include:

  7.1. Home-based psychotherapy.

    This will probably be based upon the existing model provided by clinical social workers and psychiatric nurses through visiting nurse associations. Home-based psychotherapy should emerge from two of the mechanisms expected to accompany the American Health Security Act: coverage for long-term care and an emphasis on services that are home- and community-based.

  7.2. Prevention-based services.

    This should enhance the marketability of specialties and niches built around the D.S.M.IIIR 316.00 diagnosis: Psychological factors affecting physical condition. Treatments for the 316.00 diagnostic category include stress reduction to decrease auto-immune stress reactions, for example.

    The emphasis upon prevention-based services may also open reimbursement to diagnoses that are presently nonreimbursable. At present, reimbursement eligibility is tied to medical need. Under the American Health Security Act, we can expect some reimbursement eligibility tied to the prevention of probable medical need. This may open insurance-reimbursable market niches for exercise and drug compliance counselling or smoking cessation, or even D.U.I. (Driving under the Influence education) programs.

    In recent years managed care has increasingly discouraged the kind of uncovering most theorists suggest is needed for the treatment of intensive trauma-related diagnoses such as child abuse, dissociative disorder, rape, and many forms of post-traumatic stress disorder. Under the American Health Security Act, it may be possible to obtain reimbursement for uncovering by linking it to prevention. This would probably need to be approached on a case-by-case basis, with demonstration of probable increased future functional impairment in the absence of such work.

  7.3. Minority and culturally sensitive niches.

    Mr. Gore's statement that the reform is being designed "with the special needs of the undeserved very much in mind" was in response to questions posed by representatives of Latino, Black, and Native American minority groups. Multicultural sensitivity will be even more important for all therapists' marketability.

7.4 Intensive nonresidential treatment in lieu of inpatient treatment or to shorten inpatient treatment.

Under managed care there is already a movement to replace all or parts of inpatient treatment with intensive outpatient treatment. This movement will be greatly enhanced by the emphasis under the Health Security Act on nonresidential, inpatient-alternative treatment. This change is already getting recognition from behavioral health care hospitals. Several of the large chain hospitals are now putting together their own inpatient and outpatient networks, contracting directly with employers and subcontracting with therapists for the outpatient work. In other words, they are setting up their own P.P.O.s.

If you already have or wish to formulate a specialty offering intensive nonresidential therapy to replace or reduce inpatient stays, your work should be increasingly valued in the near future. This specialty should offer mechanisms for handling emergencies easily and well. It should include a strong documentation component to demonstrate quality-based cost savings with no compromise in safety. But it should be developed specifically as intensive nonresidential treatment, not intensive outpatient treatment, since the plan allocates up to 120 days for intensive nonresidential treatment and a maximum of only 30 days for all outpatient treatment—which often will not be sufficient for a true hospital alternative program.

A COUNTERVAILING TREND

Dr. Uwe Reinhardt, the James Madison professor of political economy at the Woodrow Wilson School of Public and International Affairs, has done substantial research in international health economics. He has pointed to a pattern occurring after nationalization of health care in several countries: Many people who have the means have opted for private pay alternatives or supplements to the national health care plan.[6] The Health Security Act allows for the purchase of additional benefits through the purchase of supplemental insurance, at additional cost. It will also contain disincentives for going outside approved managed competition structures. (This will be necessary in order to keep the national plan viable. Otherwise, those with least risk would get cheaper or better services outside the plan, leaving only high-risk people in the plan.) The disincentives include greater cost to purchasers for fee-for-service options and probable reduced payment to out-of-network providers.

However, it is reasonable to expect that many high-income and even middle-income people will opt for private pay services in behavioral care — especially if the American Health Security Act plans they are offered are insufficiently inclusive or the wait for services is inordinately long (as has been the case in a number of the national health plans in other countries as well as in some capitated H.M.O. plans in the United States). This trend is already clear. For example, in California one of the major H.M.O.s offers such restricted behavioral health services and such a long waiting list that most established therapists have some of those H.M.O. members in their caseloads on a private pay basis. You may wish to market yourself to this group, which will probably be quite large once the Health Security Act has become established.

Despite great fanfare and the tremendous need for change, the Health Security Act will probably be implemented rather slowly. *Time* Magazine noted that health care is an "$800 billion a year industry that represents one-seventh of the gross domestic product."[7] Changing the direction of an industry this size is like turning a supertanker, which may take many miles to reach completion. This delay can be expected to be even more prolonged because of the intense lobbying that will probably accompany its debate in Congress. An indication of the intensity of this is suggested by A.M.A. board chairman, Raymond Scalettar, M.D., who said, "We want to know what the total package will be when the mother of all battles occurs."[8]

Even though this time lag may occur, it makes sense for you to factor in the probable impact, changes, and opportunities of the Health Security Act when you do your own business planning. Such planning needs to be as comprehensive as possible in terms of looking for the marketing opportunities that the marketplace makes available. This is a part of what we will be discussing in the final chapter, "Designing an M.C.O.-Targeted Marketing Plan."

These last two chapters, "Future Marketing—Near-term Repositioning" and "The Impact of the American Health Security Act," have made it clear that those therapists who wish to work with clients who can utilize insurance must market themselves. This marketing must be strategic and should probably be multidimensional. However, as therapists, most of us are not used to thinking in such terms. Therefore, in the next chapter we will be considering mechanisms for reframing your perception of marketing and your concept of yourself as a marketer so that this process will become more ego-syntonic.

NOTES

1. Chen, Edwin: *Los Angeles Times,* 3/30/93. Pages A1 and A24.
2. North, Ronald J., President, North, Clawson & Bolt, Ltd., presented in workshop "Health Care Reform and Behavioral Health Benefits Issues" at 1993 E.A.P.A. conference on 4/19/93. (Diagram includes slight alterations to reflect changes in the Health Security Act.)
3. Chen, Edwin: *Los Angeles Times,* 3/30/93. Pages A1 and A24.
4. Chen, Edwin. "Panel Weighing 'Luxury Tax' on Health Benefits" *Los Angeles Times,* 3/17/93. Page A14.
5. From speech given at Charter Hospital in Thousand Oaks, Ca. on 3/23/93.
6. Dr. Uwe Reinhardt in keynote speech, "The Comparison of Futurist and International Views on Health Care Reform," at the Fifth Annual National Managed Health Care Congress, 4/14/93.
7. Duffy, Michael. *"Operation Hillary"* in *Time* Magazine, 3/22/93. Page 36.
8. Beck, Melinda with Mary Hager and Rich Thomas. *"The Next Bite: Paying for Health Care." Newsweek,* 3/1/93. Page 28.

9/
Ego-Syntonic Marketing

Marketing to managed care can be a win-win activity — with you helping the managed care company accomplish its goals by aligning with a good therapist: you!

However, in all probability, the first experience the average therapist has when considering marketing to managed care is cognitive dissonance. Most of us experience some incongruity between our self concepts and the term "marketing," and we may experience further incongruity between the concept "managed care" and the term "good." Holding on to discomfort about "marketing" or about "managed care" while at the same time seeking to market one's practice to managed care is similar to trying to sail a boat with the anchor trailing along behind it.

Therefore, before actually beginning to market to managed care, you may find it extremely helpful to consider attempting a cognitive shift that might produce greater comfort with professional and ethical marketing and also with professional and ethical managed care in a managed competition environment. In this way, you can experience relatively smooth sailing when marketing to M.C.O.s.

Even the most cursory, informal survey of therapists, including those most familiar with managed care,[1] suggests that a large majority of therapists find the idea of marketing to be ego-dystonic. It is felt to be inconsistent with one's perception of self.[2] As we know, when one seeks to operate in ways that feel alien to self, the effort is usually countertherapeutic. This means that the same perceptual changes we seek to foster in our clients can become useful for us. And perceptual change is what I hope will occur as a result of this chapter!

Most psychotherapists tend to see their practice primarily in terms of an opportunity to heal and to become an advocate for psychological health. If we can expand that vision to also see our practice from a business perspective that includes marketing, some major advantages become available. The potential gains can include a more complete integration into the real world for the therapist (since psychotherapy is a business), modelling effective self-caretaking, enhanced therapeutic satisfaction (since niche marketing usually results in a caseload that is more appealing to the therapist), and increased therapeutic effectiveness (niche marketing also means that the therapist is positioning himself or herself through focusing upon the kind of work he or she does best—his or her expertise.

The business of psychotherapy usually involves some perceptual shifts regarding the issue of marketing. Therapists tend to see marketing as unprofessional and possibly unethical. We often react to the whole concept of marketing with a visceral distrust, discomfort, even disgust. Frequently, marketing is equated with sales by any means and implies unidimensional concepts of our patients (income generators) and ourselves (profit centers). Beyond that, our mentors and/or our colleagues have often indicated that we SHOULD not need to market ourselves or our practice.

These perceptions and feelings, coupled with our colleagues' views of marketing, often lead to a seemingly indissoluble ego-dystonic reaction to marketing. Part of what I hope to address in this chapter is a consideration of these elements, with the hope that an ego-syntonic position can be achieved regarding ethical marketing. We will be discussing:

1. Distinctions between marketing and sales,
2. Ways in which our present "quality service" is marketing,
3. Ethical considerations in marketing,
4. Collegial reactions to marketing,
5. The suggestion that good therapists may well have a responsibility to market themselves.

1. MARKETING VS. SELLING

The objections to marketing probably arise at least partly from a misperception of what marketing is. There is a natural tendency to react to the word "marketing" from its historical root base referring to medieval marketplaces where the buying and selling of goods took place. Therapists frequently consider "marketing" to be synonymous with "selling," and "selling" with such phenomena as advertising and telephone solicitations. And when we look at that process, it often seems that there are no boundaries around "selling." The sales process frequently seems to cross the boundaries of good taste, much less ethics. To identify one's professional business with that form of selling is uncomfortable, to say the least.

Advertising has always been suspect among professionals. Until 1977, there were outright bans on professional advertising on the basis that professions constitute a public service and therefore should be "above trade." In 1977, the United States Supreme Court ruled that state laws and bar association rules prohibiting lawyer advertising violated the free speech guarantees of the First Amendment.[3] Almost immediately, a deluge of professional advertisements appeared, a number of which were considerably lacking in taste and professionalism in the minds of many.

The concept that "marketing" implies only sales of a service to customers for a profit limits and distorts the word. The Harper *Dictionary of Modern Thoughts* refers to marketing as including a "corporate strategy (which) may include the mix and volume of products, pricing, distribution methods, guarantees and servicing, advertising and promotion, and sales force management."[4] In other words, it concerns itself with the business aspects of developing a needed or wanted service and then delivering it in such a way as to attract and satisfy clients. Therapists do not treat their patients as just customers (although patients certainly are customers). And the healing process in therapy is not seen as just another product to be sold. But it is a service, and services were exchanged in the earliest marketplaces.

2. OUR PRESENT "QUALITY SERVICE" IS MARKETING

Although marketing may seem like a foreign concept that is unappealing to therapists, one of the ways to come to terms with it and to make it more ego-syntonic is to look at how familiar it really is. Although the elements of marketing described above are couched in business terminology, a quick translation into terms that are more familiar to therapists will demonstrate that most of us have engaged in ethical marketing all along. For example, we can substitute our term "specialty" for "product mix" or "individual, conjoint, and group" for "distribution methods." This provides a hint of the range of marketing elements which are inherent in the practices of most quality-based therapy practices. Such marketing elements include:

1. Patient satisfaction initiatives,
2. Strategic planning,
3. Specialty products for market niching,
4. Competitive distribution methods,
5. Account servicing, and
6. Advertising and promotion.

Let's look at these in greater detail:

Patient Satisfaction

Usually, we simply assume that it is therapeutic to find ways of promoting the satisfaction of our patients. We do that through establishing our offices in convenient locations, providing face validity through locating in high-rise office buildings and posting our licenses, certificates, and awards in prominent places, designing our waiting rooms to be calm and comfortable spaces with relatively current reading materials, providing on-site parking, helping with insurance processing, and so forth. These all constitute forms of marketing.

Strategic Planning

Strategic planning is also an area that most therapists have given at least some thought to; here again, it is generally considered to be a plus. Yet, strategic planning is definitely a part of marketing. Often, therapists choose a location in a growing area or in an office building that has other professionals who might be inclined to refer. Frequently we join clinics as a way to obtain a greater joint impact upon our community and as a way to enhance the services we can provide over the long term. Strategic planning is evident when master's level clinicians decide to return for a doctorate or a therapist obtains the training necessary to achieve a certification.

Specialty Products for Market Niching

As suggested above, in the business of psychotherapy, the marketing term "product mix" would probably be best translated as "specialty." If we make that translation, it becomes immediately clear that therapists continuously engage in marketing through selecting specialties that constitute unique market niches. With the proliferation of new information in the field of psychotherapy, the only way to ethically serve patients well is through extensive continuing education. This continuing education produces new or enhanced specialty knowledge, which is then translated into marketing, even if in no way other than providing quality service. Specialty groups (such as those offered specifically for bereavement or for relationship-building) and specialized groups (such as multifamily groups or men's awareness groups) constitute additional elements in the product mix that therapists offer.

Competitive Distribution Methods

The primary method of distributing services in psychotherapy continues to be individual therapy. But when a therapist also offers conjoint therapy, family therapy, group therapy, or workshops he or she is providing a different, added distribution method for his product (therapy).

Account Servicing

Although we do not provide guarantees (in fact, many ethical therapists clarify this on disclosure sheets), we do service our cases. We take responsibility for patients' progress and their disposition. We refer patients to inpatient hospital programs when that becomes necessary and appropriate. We call in colleagues when needed. And we work with our patients to understand when discharge is appropriate. Many therapists go on to provide additional services such as insurance processing and even allowing a no-interest balance to be carried until the insurance comes through. All of these are ways we provide better value to our patients. In business terms this means we are "servicing our accounts" and marketing through quality.

Advertising and Promotion

Advertising and promotional activities are clearer aspects of marketing that are inherent in therapists' practice maintenance. Most therapists maintain business telephone numbers and probably most advertise them in phonebook yellow pages. It is not unusual for therapists in crowded markets to make speeches and present workshops to the public, or to serve on volunteer community boards both as a part of our commitment to the community and as a way to become more visible within the community. The fact is that the practice of psychotherapy is a business!

3. ETHICAL CONSIDERATIONS IN MARKETING

It is possible, of course, to market in an unethical way. Implying that services will be (or have been) delivered which are not, suggesting that services are needed when they are not, and accepting kickbacks for referring clients are a few of the ways marketing can be (and sometimes is) done unethically. But this book emphasizes marketing through quality and through sophisticated niche development based upon understanding the marketplace. Those are very ethical — and very needed — concepts.

4. COLLEGIAL REACTIONS TO MARKETING

One of the statements made to me when I first began private practice was, "If you are any good, patients will come to you." I have found that many other therapists were told the same thing. In retrospect it seems significant to me that this message was usually given to me by people who were not in private practice themselves.

There are many flaws in this argument that, "If you are any good, patients will come to you," and it is important to note them since if you carry such a belief it will probably undermine any marketing you do. Here are three flaws:

1. Most therapists know some colleagues who are not considered good by others in their profession. Yet those "not good" therapists continue to attract at least a few patients, and sometimes many. So, it can also be said, "If you are NOT ANY GOOD, patients will still come to you."
2. The second part of the expression "If you are any good, patients will come to you" appears to be a contradiction in terms. How can patients

come to you if they don't know you exist? The statement implies that quality will speak for itself. But for therapists to demonstrate quality, they must have an initial group of patients with whom to do quality work, and where do those people come from? Often they come from agencies, internship organizations, or other places the therapist had previously worked. But the fact is that establishing a reputation among previous colleagues and patients is a form of marketing.

3. Doing a good job is itself marketing. Probably, service quality has been used as a primary marketing tool since prehistoric times when some artists were chosen to paint wondrous animals on the walls of caves in Altamira, Spain. The dramatic quality of those paintings suggests that only the best of the clan's artists were chosen for this task. The concept that doing a good job equals new patients implies word-of-mouth marketing on the basis of quality.

5. MARKETING MAY BE A PROFESSIONAL RESPONSIBILITY

At the beginning of Chapter 3, I noted a painful scenario of therapists who have established good working relationships with patients and then lost those patients because the therapist did not have a contract with the patient's new managed care insurer. This scenario has occurred in disproportionate numbers to established, high quality clinicians whom I know. This has happened because those therapists often had satisfactory practices and saw no need to pursue managed care contracts. When they finally did, the provider lists were full. The result has been that in many cases patients have ended up with treatment from less skilled therapists while some of the most capable therapists have fewer patients. Marketing is the answer to that paradox. Please consider that if you have worked to become the very best at what you do, and nobody knows, then your capability is irrelevant. And your potential patients will end up seeing someone who is less capable. So you owe it to them as well as to yourself to market your practice!

In the next chapter you will find a format for designing your own M.C.O.-targeted marketing plan. As you go through that, I suggest that you consider it from the perspective of a marketer—but a professional and ethical marketer. As you consider each aspect of the plan, ask yourself if it is something you would be proud to hold up as professional and ethical. By building on the concepts found in the rest of the book, you will have no difficulty in developing ethical and professional elements. And then you will have produced a form of marketing you can be proud to own. This kind of marketing is very ego-syntonic.

NOTES

1. This refers to an informal survey of therapists who attended the Behavioral Healthcare Tomorrow Conference on behavioral managed care, sponsored by the Institute for Behavioral Healthcare in Chicago, IL. September 8–13, 1992.
2. *Psychiatric Dictionary Fourth Edition* by Leland E. Hinsie, M.D. and Robert Jean Campbell, M.D. Oxford University Press. New York. 1970. Page 251.
3. *"Building a Successful Professional Practice with Advertising"* by Irwin Braun. Publisher: AMACOM. 1981. Page 1.
4. The Harper Dictionary of Modern Thought, edited by Alan Bullock and Oliver Stallybrass. Harper and Row, San Francisco, CA. 1977. Page 370.

10/
Designing an M.C.O.-Targeted Marketing Plan

Throughout this book, we have considered many concepts and suggestions for marketing to managed care in a variety of ways. The purpose of this chapter is to pull all of that together into a nine-element marketing plan which has three purposes. It is designed specifically for psychotherapists. It is targeted to the managed care marketplace. And it is designed to be molded by you to fit yourself, personally. The nine elements are:

1. A personal priorities analysis,
2. A competitive analysis of the field,
3. A competitive analysis of the local competition,
4. A revenue, time, and energy budget,
5. A business goals statement,
6. Strategies for competitive positioning,
7. A mission statement,
8. Tasks for implementing the competitive positioning and for reaching the goals, and finally
9. A time-line for reaching those goals.

The first four elements are important precursors to a business goals statement because they define its context and its boundaries. Even though you will probably go back and change some of the material later, this information is absolutely essential in order to keep your marketing plan workable for you personally and realistic in terms of the overall business conditions in which it must operate. Since your business goal will be limited by the competitive environment, you must formulate strategies for distinguishing yourself from similar competitors. Therefore, the sixth element will be critical to your success. Once you have looked at your goals and strategies, you will be able to formulate a mission statement, which is basically a public pronouncement of your beliefs, your business goals, your strengths, and your special characteristics or niches. Next, it is necessary to translate all of this into straightforward tasks that can be realistically implemented. And finally, those tasks should be placed in a time-line you can use to measure your progress and to motivate and structure yourself.

REVIEW

In this chapter, we will discuss each of these nine elements in turn. However, let us begin by reviewing some of the points made so far in the book about these nine marketing plan elements.

In Chapter 1, we discussed the vertical nature of the behavioral health care financing system. This flow of financing and power speaks to the importance of making careful choices among managed care partners. It also suggests that market niches should be as meaningful as possible to those who have power along that vertical network—decision makers such as gatekeepers or benefits managers. (One mechanism we discussed for aligning with the decision makers was developing niches that reduce the M.C.O.'s service delivery cost.) As you undertake the strategizing part of your marketing plan, this understanding of where power lies and who will become the ultimate purchaser or rejector of your services will be critical.

Chapter 1 also outlined seven process steps therapists can take to market themselves within the behavioral health care financing system. The present chapter deals with step 7, "Market your package to M.C.O.s." But as we go through the strategies for competitive positioning, you will want to remember steps 4, 5, 6 which suggest that you develop a service or skill edge, package it, and focus carefully on specific managed care companies for your marketing pitch.

In Chapter 6, we discussed the desirability of developing a marketing plan that is specific, thoughtful, planned, strategic, and goal-directed. That chapter concentrated on strategic choices that are specific, thoughtful, and planned. This chapter will pick up from that point and go on to emphasize the procedures for designing and implementing an M.C.O.-targeted market plan that is narrowly focused upon specific goals.

In Chapter 7, we looked at the evolving structures of behavioral health care delivery systems. From that, it is clear that provider group contracting should become an increasingly important part of the behavioral health care service delivery picture in the near future. This leaves you with a choice between (1) becoming an H.M.O. staff employee or a group subcontractor, (2) honing an extremely focused private practice pitched to particular managed care companies, (3) becoming a principal in a provider group practice, or (4) some combination or variation on the above three options. Both the complications and the potential for stability for these options were considered in Chapter 7, and these must come into play as you make your decision about the individual business goals that will fit best for you personally.

In Chapter 8, we considered the probable changes that will occur in the near future as a result of the American Health Security Act and we looked at a number of niche options that could position you favorably to take advantage of those changes. In this chapter, you will be encouraged to pick some of those that fit for you and to develop niches that should play well in the managed competition environment of the American Health Security Act. And you will be asked to draw up a market plan around them.

PLANNING: AN ILLOGICAL PROGRESSION

Those of us who have worked with managed care are very familiar with goal-setting and treatment planning. We know that in reality this process is not as logical or clear as it appears on paper. This chapter will help you formulate a progression for setting personal marketing plans that is relatively logical but folds back upon itself.

As you consider one part of the plan and make tentative decisions about it, those decisions and considerations will have implications for other parts. So I suggest that you go about this planning process with several screens or windows on your computer or with several pieces of paper, a *pencil* (not a pen), and a large eraser. In this way, you can alter and change as you go. Allow yourself to make tentative decisions and modify those as you go along. Of course, up to a certain point this openness to change should extend into the execution of the plan so that you can take advantage of opportunities that present themselves along the way.

1. PERSONAL PRIORITIES ANALYSIS

Although you will probably find it useful to push yourself somewhat by setting business goals that stretch your capabilities, it is also very important to be harshly realistic. As therapists, we are all familiar with what happens when a person decides that he SHOULD be achieving at a level that stretches his capabilities too far. And we all know of the interpersonal breakups that can occur when one sets business goals that result in the neglect of one's significant other.

Realistically, your final plan will not be exclusively goal-driven. It must also be investment-driven. As we will see in the competitive analysis sections and in the budget section, some business goals require prodigious amounts of time and energy in addition to money. But there is a wide range of possible courses with an accompanying wide range of investments attached to them. So it is extremely important for you to be as clear as possible about how you want this to fit into your life.

Most private practice therapists have gone into the field in order to enrich their own lives as well as the lives of others. We have usually found that the time, energy, and financial commitments necessary to make that happen have been worthwhile. Usually, we fall into a progression of priorities in our lives that work pretty well. But in recent years, the changes in our profession — as in many other professions — have increasingly forced us to look again at where the priorities lie, because the professional parts are consuming more and more.

If you have not already done so, this is a time to take stock of your priorities. I suggest the following exercise:

1. Look at what is most important to you — family, spiritual life, recreation, community, fun, or work? Probably it is a combination of those elements and more.
2. Make a list of the 10 things which are most important to you.
3. Prioritize that list in descending order of importance. If work is not on the list, that fact is very important. Make a note of that and then add work at the very bottom of the list.
4. Look at where work is on your list.
5. Now consider what work means to you. Does it mean a livelihood? It usually does, of course. If so, is that all it means? In the somewhat unlikely event that the answer to this question is not immediately

clear to you, one way to determine whether or not work means nothing more than a livelihood is to imagine that you have just won a lottery and no longer have to work. Would you continue doing so anyway? What else does work give you? Is it intellectual challenge, an opportunity to be of service or to make an important change in the world or in someone's world, prestige, an antidote to boredom, a way to fill time, all of these, or combinations of these? What happens when you replace the term "work" with the term "profession"?

6. Ask yourself how well a private practice geared primarily to managed care fits with your personality. Are you a self-starter and relatively comfortable with risk or do you prefer a more comfortable or laid-back lifestyle?

7. Once you have considered the questions in number 6, go back and look again at where work should fall on your priority list. Change its position if a change is indicated.

Now you have a priority list for your life! And you have an idea of where work falls on that list. Please keep this in front of you as you progress through the rest of your marketing plan. It will be especially important to have this available when you reach step 4 (making a revenue, time, and energy budget), because you will probably be forced to trade off priorities and to do a great deal of compromising.

2. COMPETITIVE ANALYSIS OF THE FIELD

The marketing plan outlined in this chapter suggests a different order and a different emphasis than is usually utilized. Most marketing plans relegate the competitive analysis phase to the third or fourth element and focus primarily upon competitor analysis rather than upon market analysis. I believe that in our field these choices need to be changed. To my mind, a competitive analysis of the field is more important than competitor analysis—although some competitor analysis should be done as well. It should not be the third or forth element to be considered in compiling a marketing plan; it should stand immediately after the analysis of your personal life priorities in the marketing planning process.

This primacy is dictated by a central fact that has become one of the most important developments in our profession. As with many other professional fields in the United States today, the present behavioral health care delivery system is marked by an enormous inequity. The number of very well qualified psychotherapist providers vastly exceeds the number of therapists needed by M.C.O.s, except in isolated geographic locations. Generally, it is a buyer's market for M.C.O.s. This inequity distorts the balance between buyer and seller and affects every area of the marketing plan, as you probably know at this point from personal experience. This oversupply will limit and hone your options. It dictates the need to specialize into a market niche and it strongly argues for a client-driven rather than a seller-driven marketing strategy.

This book has emphasized the primacy of managed care in the present behavioral health care delivery system. The proposals for national health care suggest that managed care's primacy will continue. Even though you may be tempted to conclude that the private practice of psychotherapy is on its way out or to conclude that you must scramble to obtain any managed care contract you can, the purpose of this book is to present a more optimistic strategy.

I believe that it is possible for you to position yourself to work comfortably with a few value-based M.C.O.s by emphasizing quality-based psychotherapy. This requires restructuring your practice to emphasize quality the way quality is understood by M.C.O.s, while retaining your professional ethics that require that the needs of the patient are to be considered first. In most cases, it means initially contracting with a number of managed care companies that do not, in fact, fall on the higher end of the value-based mix. This will be necessary so that you can position yourself in the marketplace and discover which M.C.O.s truly emphasize high value and which M.C.O.s just say they are high-value companies because it sounds good to say that. It will be necessary in order for you to experience whether or not you can work efficiently and comfortably with the companies under consideration.

In this way, just as M.C.O.s are profiling providers, you can profile the M.C.O.s and end up with behavioral health care delivery partners who fit well for you. Later in your plan, you will be setting goals. This part of your plan should anticipate your goal-setting to define the characteristics of the M.C.O.s you ultimately wish to position yourself with as your primary business partners. This is also the time to look at diversity of practice arrangements and what the trends are for the near and long-term future (see Chapter 7).

What this means is that the next piece in your marketing planning is to get as clear an understanding as possible of the marketplace (nationally, locally, and personally) and of the near-term trends as they are likely to affect you. This is necessary so that you can base your goals in reality. I suggest the following steps:

1. Set out nine pages (or windows on your computer) with headings of the nine business elements: Personal priorities analysis (which you have already compiled), Field analysis, Competition analysis, Budget, Goal statement, Positioning strategies, Mission statement, Tasks, and Time line.
2. Review Chapter 1 "Coming to Terms with Managed Care," Chapter 6 "Strategic Positioning: Targeting Your M.C.O. Partners," and Chapter 7 "Future Marketing: Near-term Repositioning." Write down the tentative implications for each of the nine elements in your marketing plan.
3. You should now have some raw data for generating ideas on each of the marketing plan elements. More important for the purposes of this section, you should have some beginning ideas of where you can and want to fit into this field and what will be required to get there. Take another sheet of paper and list the following questions:

   A. What are the advantages/disadvantages of staying in private practice vs. subcontracting with a group or becoming an H.M.O. staff employee?
   B. If I stay in (or go into) private practice, where do I want to position my practice? (When you answer this question and question C below, you may wish to review the criteria we discussed in Chapter 6 "Strategic Positioning: Targeting Your M.C.O. Partners.")
   C. Which managed care organizations do I want to affiliate with: None? Low cost? High quality? Value-based? Any I can get into initially and specific ones later?
   D. What opportunities does the present behavioral health care marketplace open up for me, now and potentially?
   E. What constraints does the present behavioral health care marketplace impose upon my practice, now and potentially?

3. COMPETITIVE ANALYSIS OF THE LOCAL COMPETITION

Think about the special characteristics of your local area, and begin to ask yourself some more questions:

A. Are there many therapists or only a few? What are the implications of this for my practice, both now and potentially?

B. Is managed care well established or is it only beginning to come to my locality? What are the implications of this for my practice, now and potentially?

C. Has one local agency, clinic, or Independent Practice Association wrapped up most of the managed care business (which will require my affiliating with them or fighting harder for new contracts) or is it a fairly open contracting field? (Again, write down the implications for your practice both for the present and the future.)

D. Are there underserved localities, specialties, or minorities in my area? If so, how can that be utilized in terms of a market niche or specialized positioning?

E. Are there any other questions that could be helpful to my planning?

4. REVENUE, TIME, AND ENERGY BUDGET

This is a time to ponder! Go back to the personal priorities you established in section 1 above. Think particularly about how much time and energy you can put into your marketing plan. In terms of your present commitments and the priorities you set, how much time can you realistically commit to the furtherance of your marketing plan? One hour per week? Ten? Twenty?

In looking at how much time is available to invest in business development, most clinicians will feel squeezed. They must consider what they can invest beyond the time they are already spending on direct clinical work, continuing education, and paperwork. Of course, an employee or subcontractor position usually involves little or no business development time. Group practice principles may devote very small amounts of time (as little as one or two hours per week) if others are hired or delegated to do it, or they may spend very high amounts of time. In medical and legal group practices, it is not unusual for some principals to devote their full time to the group's business development. But in many behavioral health group practices clinicians spend as much as 20 hours per week doing business development in addition to their direct clinical time. Any clinician who wishes to maintain a viable private practice in a managed care environment should commit himself to a minimum of four hours per week of business development—and he will probably need substantially more.

Unless you are able to contract out for others to do your business development, if you end up with a genuine capability and/or commitment of only one or two hours per week, you should probably skip over some of this material, which anticipates contracting with M.C.O.s on a private practice basis. Since it can take up to an hour to process some managed care applications and around a half hour just to inspect contracts to assure legal safety, you will probably not have the time to make a managed care-based private practice work well. It will probably make more sense for you to contract for a paid position with a staff H.M.O. or a subcontractor position with a provider group.

If you have a private practice now, you could maintain that practice with decreasingly available indemnity patients as long as possible and then move into a paid position. Or you might consider maintaining a small private practice composed of easily obtained (but decreasingly available) indemnity patients and easily obtained managed care patients. This could be done either on a stand-alone basis or in conjunction with a paid position, depending upon your need or wish for income.

If you can commit to four hours per week or more, you can probably make a marketing plan work on a private practice basis or on the basis of operating as a principal in a provider group, should either of those alternatives appeal to you.

Think also about your energy. Each of us has our own circadian rhythms, and most of us are better toward the beginning of our workday than after we have done a great deal of work and are exhausted, physically or mentally. Of course, your plan will be more effective if you can commit to working on it during your high energy time rather than when you can squeeze it in or at the end of a long workday.

Revenue is the third critical investment resource to be considered in the formation of an investment plan. I suggest that you begin by looking at your overall budget and see what you can afford. Perhaps you already have a marketing budget, since various forms of paid marketing—especially advertising—have been helpful in the past. Since advertising is much less useful in a primarily managed care environment, perhaps some of those funds could be diverted to your new managed care-targeted marketing plan.

Probably, a commitment of as little as $75.00 per month would be sufficient to get you started toward relatively small expenses such as periodicals and newsletters. But this would slow down and severely limit your plan over the long run, since only the least expensive meetings could be included and personal marketing consultation would probably be unaffordable. An alternative might be to invest a relatively small amount (such as $75.00 or $100.00 per month) initially, but to commit yourself to investing more later as your income increases. One mechanism for doing this is to project what your income will be in the future if current trends in your practice continue. (Be realistic and recognize that if the trends are for a decrease, that is what should be projected.) Then keep track of your income, with the expectation that the beginning stages of your market plan will push it past present projections at some point. When your income begins to exceed present projections, you can then devote all (or significant portions) of that "excess" income to your marketing plan. In this way the marketing plan would become fully operational only after it has begun to pay for itself.

5. STATEMENT OF BUSINESS GOALS

This is the place to pull all of the material developed above in the first four steps into one statement. I suggest that you begin by making the very important choice of how you will operate in this marketplace. Now that you have developed the information from sections 1 to 4, you logically come to three major choices, with many gradations between those choices:

A. Group Subcontractor or H.M.O. Staff Employee

If you do not wish (or cannot afford) to spend any or very much energy, time, or money on marketing your practice, you should consider becoming a staff member or employee of a health maintenance organization or becoming a group subcontractor. That choice usually produces a limited income, but it requires little or no investment, carries limited risk, and provides relatively high stability (though subcontractors are the first to go from provider groups when the finances get tight).

B. Private Practice

Private practice is probably the best choice If you can invest substantial time and moderate energy, but a limited amount of money. That choice can produce a moderately high income (in the low six figures). It carries moderate risk, and usually provides some stability—though one often has to scramble to keep it stable.

C. Principal in a Group Practice

As was indicated in Chapter 7, group practices can be structured in a variety of ways. However, the major purpose of a group practice is to contract for the group participants with preferred provider organizations and self-insured corporations. In both of those cases the majority of the contracts—and often the most lucrative contracts—are those that require some provider financial risk, such as capitation. This risk, plus the cost of group formation and maintenance (overhead, legal fees, utilization review malpractice insurance, computerization, etc.), make group practice a very expensive choice financially and usually in terms of time. If structured correctly, it can also be very financially rewarding. Therefore, group practice is the direction you should consider if your goals are for high stability and high financial reward and you can afford to invest large amounts of time and money into practice development.

Since group practices are often marketed by specialized marketing and legal firms that concentrate on business development and contracting, a further discussion of marketing for group practices would require too much space for this volume. But since you are still reading this book you have probably at least tentatively decided against becoming an H.M.O. employee or a group subcontractor in favor of marketing your private practice. Therefore, the remainder of this chapter will be devoted to the formation and execution of an M.C.O.-targeted plan to market your private practice.

If the logical progression of your personal goals leads you to conclude that private practice is the way you wish to market yourself to managed care companies, the next step consists of actually starting to write down the goals statement. I suggest that you proceed in the following manner:

1. Initial Goals

Define your initial goals by looking at the material you developed in section 1 above (Personal Priorities Analysis), section 2 (Competitive Analysis of the Field), and section 3 (Competitive Analysis of the Local Competition).

2. Investments

Look at what you can invest in business development (section 4: Revenue, Time, and Energy Budget).

3. Intermediate Goals Statement

Redefine your initial goals to arrive at intermediate goals through compromise. Consider whether the time, money, and energy you have available to invest are sufficient to achieve what you want. They probably will not be, so you will probably have to sacrifice elsewhere to put in more time and money or you will have to alter the initial goals you set for your practice.

Try to state your goals as concretely as possible. For example, you may start by saying, "I am willing to devote substantial time and a little money to obtain a stable, solo practice that will provide a moderate income over the long term." Try to clarify and concretize that statement with something like:

> My goal is to develop a practice with long-term stability consisting of 25 to 30 client hours per week, producing an average of $6,000.00 gross income per month, derived from three to six preferred provider M.C.O. contracts with companies that demonstrate their stability with large size, insurance ownership, and emphasis on value. I am willing to invest at least $100.00 per month and 15 hours per week in business development. As my income increases, I am willing to sacrifice up to $1,500.00 per month of that increase for as long

as six months at a time in order to continuously reposition myself with M.C.O.s so that I can reach my goals.

6. STRATEGIES FOR COMPETITIVE POSITIONING

Once you have at least a beginning clarification of your goals, it is time to strategize the mechanisms for achieving them. It is particularly important at this point to go back to sections 2 and 3 above to look at the competitive environment you must operate within. In most cases, you will have to clearly differentiate yourself from the other psychotherapists in your area.

You will probably find it useful to start by looking at how you marketed yourself to indemnity patients. Often you will be able to utilize some of the same marketing advantages. But there are some significant differences. Managed care decision makers are more difficult to reach and they are much more sophisticated about therapy than has been the average consumer in the past. So do position yourself from your traditional strengths.

There are some caveats to consider however. Avoid fad diagnoses or treatment regimens. Avoid marketing yourself through expertise with diagnoses or treatments that suggest long-term care unless you can demonstrate a cost containment advantage. With those provisos, do find market niches that emphasize your strengths or contain costs, or increase value, or address special needs of the M.C.O.'s purchasers (benefit managers) or patient populations (example: African-American therapists or lesbian therapists or therapists who are fluent in Spanish). As this suggests, a review of Chapters 2, 3, and 4 will give you a variety of ideas regarding how to differentiate yourself for a market advantage.

The primary thrust of Chapter 5 was quality. Even though that chapter concerned itself primarily with retention on the active list of providers, it can be extremely useful as you seek ways to increase your competitive position. Developing and maintaining a quality-based business will not differentiate you immediately, especially if you get a string of particularly difficult cases (as the author did with one M.C.O. recently). But over a period of time it will pay off in providing you with a market advantage, so I suggest that you utilize quality as a marketing tool. One way to achieve that is to turn to the quality checklist in Chapter 5 and determine how much of it you can implement in your practice. Then market it!

Now you may wish to go back and update your goals statement with strategies included. An example of how it might now read is as follows:

> My goal is to develop a practice with long-term stability consisting of 25 to 30 client hours per week producing an average of $6,000.00 gross income per month, derived from three to six preferred provider M.C.O. contracts with companies which demonstrate their stability through large size, insurance ownership, and emphasis on value. I am willing to invest at least $100.00 per month and 15 hours per week in business development. As my income increases, I am willing to sacrifice up to $1,500.00 per month of that increase for as long as six months at a time in order to continuously reposition myself with M.C.O.s so that I can reach my goals. My strategy is to develop a quality-driven practice utilizing the quality checklist except for items 74 and 75 (see Chapter 5), my capability with sign language, and a developing market niche in somatoform pain disorder. I will aggressively market as many managed care companies as I can find until I have 10 active contracts and then I will gradually cull my contracts to just those most satisfying and remunerative to work with.

7. MISSION STATEMENT

Now you have sufficient information with which to formulate a mission statement. The mission statement is the way you define your practice and its purpose. In other words it should be the "headline" of your public relations.[1] This will be a distillation of your personal priorities and commitments, your business goals, and your strategies. It represents the way you will frame your work both verbally and in writing to anyone who asks. In the mission statement you should include what you do, how you differ from others, and who your customers are—in this case, managed care companies. The mission statement should be brief and clear. Therefore, you should take some time in formulating it. As an example, based upon the examples we have used so far, the mission statement might read as follows:

> I am a psychotherapist with _____ years of training. I utilize sign language and have the skills needed to work with a wide range of patients on a goal-oriented, time-limited basis through major managed care companies. And I am particularly concerned with people who experience somatoform pain.

This statement can be used in a variety of ways. Its primary use will be to introduce you; whether that introduction is one you do verbally to a crowded room or one appearing in a cover letter to a managed care company.

8. TASKS FOR IMPLEMENTING THE COMPETITIVE POSITIONING AND FOR REACHING THE GOALS

This is the time to begin laying out just how your goals will be implemented. It will be helpful to begin by reviewing some of the material on the seven pages (or windows) you have completed so far. On your sheet "Competitive Analysis of the Field," review questions 2 and 3. On your sheet "Competitive Analysis of the Local Competition," review all of the questions. Review your last goals statement and the strategies for competitive positioning. As you do so, write down the tasks it will take to implement them. For each of those tasks, trace back and write down what task has to precede the present one in order for it to get accomplished in an orderly progression. Now you are ready to assign time periods to each task completion so that they can all sum together to accomplish the end goal in an expeditious manner.

9. TIME-LINE FOR REACHING GOALS— AN EXAMPLE

Setting up a time-line basically consists of setting very clear goals, considering what needs to get accomplished to meet those goals, and setting dates for meeting those intermediate accomplishments. These dates then become markers or signposts that one has come a particular distance toward getting to the final goal. To illustrate, let us look at one possible time-line. You may not want to accomplish all of what will be discussed here. But this example can give you some ideas. I encourage you to utilize the parts that fit for you. In this example of time-line planning, we will be discussing

(A) goal setting, (B) financial projection, (C) time commitment, (D) time-plan markers, and (E) task-time allocation.

A. Goal Setting

As therapists we know about the dynamics of setting and working toward goals, so we have some advantages in this process. I encourage you to think about the suggestions you would make to your patients and then implement them for yourself. Part of what you would probably suggest would be the use of intense focus and visualization. Once you begin setting your business goals, it is a good idea to set aside a particular time each day to meditate upon and visualize your goals. Meditation can be used to ponder each aspect of the goal and to try it on for a feeling of whether or not it fits or needs adjustments. Consider the old adage: "Be careful about what you ask for. You might get it." Sometimes what one thinks one wants initially does not truly fit in the end. This initial personal-professional goal-setting time is the point at which to deeply understand the implications of each aspect of your goals and insure that they meet your lifestyle needs.

Coinciding with meditation is visualization. Visualization of their goals has been used by athletes to compete more effectively in many sports ever since the concept was popularized for golf through J. Heise in 1961.[2] As you begin to clearly define your goals, it can help you to imagine achieving them. That means to imagine seeing them, feeling them, hearing them, and wearing them in the sense of going through a period of time in your mind feeling as you will when you have accomplished them, recognizing the consequences and how those consequences will alter your life. Doing this kind of meditation and visualization for 10–15 minutes at the same time each day over some months (or even weeks) can enhance your motivation and focus your energy for meeting the goals.

B. Financial Projection

The next step is to clarify your financial investment over the lifetime of your marketing plan. I suggest that you begin with a financial projection, so that you can determine when your income increases. There are two reasons this information will be valuable to you: (1) It will let you know when your marketing plan has reached the point of beginning to pay off, and (2) it will let you know how much income can be diverted into the marketing plan. Understanding how close you are getting to a payoff is critical, because it is hard to keep motivated over the period of time that will probably be necessary. To give you an idea of how critical this is, please notice your own reaction to the next sentence: Realistically, any meaningful payoff from marketing to managed care companies will probably not occur for at least six months, and it is usually closer to a year and a half.

There will be many mechanisms for determining that you are beginning to have success in this effort: contacts made, applications obtained and accepted, contracts signed, and clients referred. But, as you know, the final payoff will not come until you bill and then receive payment for seeing those clients. Increased income is the final arbiter of success in your marketing plan. I strongly encourage you to look at and even chart the other indicators (number of contracts signed, for example) because you will need intermediate motivators. In all likelihood, however, you will want to designate the final step of payment as the critical measure of success. If you expect to obtain this income differential in less than a year and a half, you will probably be unfair to yourself and to your marketing efforts, and end up feeling less successful than you really are.

The second reason for income projection is to let you know when additional funds can be diverted into your marketing plan. Many therapists may conclude that it is prudent—or necessary—to commit only a minimum initial investment into an M.C.O.-targeted marketing plan, and will decide upon something in the range of $100.00 per month. But a fully operational marketing plan to managed care companies should utilize considerably more than that. Although you can start out with expenditures limited to newsletter subscriptions and local meetings, you will find it advantageous to begin attending at least one national conference as soon as possible. Those cost around $1,000.00 for the combination of tuition, hotel, and air fare, but they are invaluable both for contacts and for information about near-term and long-term movements in the managed care field. Therefore, it can work well for you to make minimal initial expenditures of seed money into your plan, but to also designate as an investment into your marketing plan a certain amount of any funds received in excess of your projected gross income expectations.

Income averaging for financial projection can be quite simple. For any particular month, just go back and look at the amount of income you took in for that same month during each of the past five years. If you notice a percentage increase—or decrease—over those years, include that in a projection for probable income during that month this year. The resulting figure is an estimate of what you can expect if everything remains the same in your practice. Since private practice income is strongly effected by a variety of short-term factors, you may prefer to do an income projection on a quarterly or even six-month basis for greater accuracy.

C. Clarify Time Commitment

Now it is necessary to go back to your goal statement and define your time commitment more concretely. The example we used above was for 15 hours per week. But you may be able to devote more — or less. Try to start with a commitment to a specific time period each week. This may be all in one day or during the same hours over several days each week. Try to schedule at least some of those hours during your peak energy times during the day so that you can maximize your efforts. Each of us has slightly different circadian rhythms, which result in different periods of peak effectiveness. You should know yours. Emphasize marketing during at least a part of that time. Also schedule some of that time during normal business hours. Keep in mind time zone differences in other parts of the country, because you will probably end up needing to call M.C.O.s in different time zones. Be flexible about your time. If a valuable meeting will be held at an inconvenient time, try to change your schedule to accommodate it.

D. Time-Plan Markers

Once you have clarity about your financial and time commitments, you are prepared to begin laying out your time plan markers. You begin this process by delineating all of the tasks needed to reach your goals. You will find that there are hierarchies of these tasks, with some being obvious and major and others constituting minor, subsidiary elements. Your marketing plan should become a system of ascending tasks, each leading into the next. It is similar to a large river system like the Mississippi river, with all of its tributaries. By the time the Mississippi reaches Saint Louis, it has received major inflows from the Illinois, Des Moines, Wisconsin, St. Croix, and Minneapolis rivers. When it gets to New Orleans the Red, Arkansas, and Ohio have made major contributions. But there are over 250 tributaries in all and — just as important — each of the major rivers just named has its own numerous tributaries that together drain a major part of the continental United States and contribute to the massive flows of water ultimately reaching the Gulf of Mexico. In the same way, the successful completion of many tasks and of their subsidiary tasks contributes to the final success of your ultimate business goals. These fit together in the same manner that the various major rivers, minor rivers, streams and brooks fit into the final volume of water discharging from the Mississippi into the Gulf.

E. Task-Time Allocation

In defining tasks, look at your goals and define every task that appears to be needed to reach them. Also look at your present situation and its inherent opportunities. Now write down everything you might be able to do to further the possibility of obtaining your goals. Once you have listed all of these tasks, the major ones will stand out. Now list these separately. At this point you will be prepared to begin your initial time-line around major tasks. It helps to start from both ends of your marketing plan— working back from your goals and working forward from the present. We will discuss (a) working from the goal backward, (b) working from the present forward, and (c) filling in the implementing steps.

(a) From the goal backwards

If your goal is to obtain a good flow of referrals from three to six M.C.O.s, you should probably obtain contracts with at least three times that many. This is because some of the M.C.O.s with which you contract will never get good contracts from corporations in your area and some will never begin to use you for a flow of referrals because of their own idiosyncracies and flukes. That leaves a need to contract with around 18 M.C.O.s. And the contracts must be made within the next six months in order to generate a flow of referrals by one and a half years from now, because it takes time for the M.C.O.s to obtain their own corporate contracts and then to gear up to referring on a continuous basis. This means you need to establish an intermediate goal of contracting with 18 managed care companies within the next six months. The six-month goal means applying for contracts within four months. And your four month goal means finding the companies within three months.

Finding the companies means information gathering. Therefore, you should consider going to the most readily available meetings (Employee Assistance Providers Association) and subscribing to newsletters and periodicals. Since the E.A.P.A. meetings occur once a month and require getting to know people before you can get much M.C.O. information, this deadline requires attending the first E.A.P.A. meeting this month and that means finding out when and where it is within the next week. Since periodicals usually are monthlies, a similar situation occurs. You should begin sending for subscriptions within the next week in order to have the information you need within three months. Now you can see the following progression of time-lines for active M.C.O. referrals within 18 months, working backward from the goal date:

One week:
   Subscribe to periodicals
   Locate E.A.P.A. meeting and make reservation.

One month:
   Attend the first E.A.P.A. meeting.
   Begin scanning periodicals for relevant managed care companies.

Four months:
   Complete and file applications for contracts with 18 M.C.O.s.

Six months:
   Contract with 18 managed care companies.

Eighteen months:
   Target date for goal of flow of referrals from three to six managed care
      companies.

(b) From the present forward

You can also work from the present forward on time-plan markers. For example, you know that you want to target M.C.O.s that have contracts (or stand a good chance of getting contracts in the near future) with large employers in your geographic area. Therefore, it may be prudent to attend meetings (or join) the local Chamber of Commerce. You may wish to make this a part of your marketing plan and construct a time-line around this effort. The time-line could read as follows: (1) Within four days call a friend who belongs to the Chamber and who might be willing to take you as a guest and introduce you. (2) Attend their next meeting, which is scheduled for next week. (3) Ask at the meeting who could inform you about the managed care arrangements of four local major employers. (4) Seek to obtain information about the managed care arrangements of four major employers within three months. This scenario yields the following time-line:

Four days:
   Ask a friend to bring you to a Chamber of Commerce meeting.

One week:
   Attend a Chamber of Commerce meeting.
   Find out who has the information about the managed care arrangements of four large employers in your area.

Three months:
   Determine which managed care companies hold contracts with at least four major employers in your area.

(c) Filling in the implementing steps

Minor tasks should also be included in your marketing plan. Using the Mississippi analogy we spoke of before, these tasks are comparable to the Scioto, Mahoning, and Hocking rivers which flow into the Ohio. For example, the quality of your applications to M.C.O.s can be critical to the number of referrals that may be generated to you from those companies. It may also even affect whether or not you will be accepted on their panel of providers. Therefore, a series of tasks for preparing to complete the application can be fruitful. Even before an application comes into your office, you can (1) compile an expertise validation packet (see Chapter 4), (2) think through how you will word your treatment philosophy statement, (3) obtain hospital privileges, and/or (4) obtain chemical dependency or brief treatment training.

The compilation of an expertise validation packet requires paperwork primarily and the wording of a treatment philosophy statement requires a fair amount of time for thought. But both of these are tasks you can probably do almost any time you are in your office — or in your home if that is where you keep training records. It makes sense to do these at times when another task is not pressing. If you prefer working some hours outside the normal workday, these are ideal task choices because they will probably involve no phone contacts to outside sources. Therefore, give yourself a relatively long time-line with the understanding that these are in-between tasks.

On the other hand, obtaining hospital privileges may entail getting a consensus from your colleagues of which hospitals in your local area work most with M.C.O.s, getting a site visit, completing staff privilege application forms, and waiting for the application to be processed at the hospital. Getting brief therapy or chemical dependency training means finding and then wading through many brochures, scheduling the training, and taking it.

In the first example regarding goal time-lines, we targeted four months as the goal time for sending at least 15 applications to obtain managed care contracts. You can now go back and flesh out the tasks of that four months with some sub-tributary efforts and some time-plan markers based upon the present-forward time-line planning method just discussed. The new time-line tasks that integrate all of this might appear as follows:

Four days:

> Ask a friend to bring you to a Chamber of Commerce meeting.
> Begin asking colleagues about which local behavioral health hospitals work well with managed care companies.
> Peruse brochures for a chemical dependency course.

One week:

> Attend a Chamber of Commerce meeting.
> Find out who has the information about the managed care arrangements of four large employers in your area.
> Subscribe to periodicals
> Locate E.A.P.A. meeting and make reservations.

Two weeks:

> Contact at least one hospital regarding staff privileges.
> Find a chemical dependency training course and enroll in it.
> Begin work on formulating a treatment philosophy statement.

Four weeks:

> Attend the first E.A.P.A. meeting.
> Begin scanning periodicals for relevant managed care companies.
> Make a site visit to a behavioral health hospital and pick up a privileges application packet.

Six weeks:

> Apply for staff privileges at at least one behavioral health hospital which is managed care sophisticated.

Eight weeks:

> Find at least five managed care companies and request applications.

Ten weeks:

> Complete any M.C.O. applications that have come in.
> Find at least five more M.C.O.s and request applications (bringing the total to 10).

Three months:
  Complete any M.C.O. applications that have come in.
  Determine from at least four major employers which M.C.O.s they use.
  Find eight more M.C.O.s and request applications (bringing the total to 18).

14 weeks:
  Take a chemical dependency training course.
  Complete and update expertise validation packet to include the chemical
    dependency training course.

Four months:
  Complete applications for all 18 of the needed M.C.O. contracts by the end
    of this month.

   You can see that task demands begin to accumulate quickly. You should
try to be flexible, with a consistent recognition of task precedence (i.e.,
remembering that certain tasks must be completed before others can begin).
A relatively easy way to juggle all of this is to keep a tickler card file whose
date completion positions can be easily changed.

A CLOSING NOTE

   Now you have in front of you a clear, concise plan for marketing yourself
to managed care companies. It isn't easy. But worthwhile things rarely are
easy. Along the way you have probably come to know yourself better. You
have probably looked at your practice more carefully as well. And you have
probably grown because of the effort.
   Good luck! I wish you well in this endeavor for the sake of your patients
and of the behavioral health care industry. . .and of your own future.

NOTES

  1. Karlson, David, Ph.D., *"Marketing Your Consulting or Professional Services"* Crisp
    Publications, Inc. Los Altos, Ca. Page 9.
  2. Heise, J. *"How you can play better golf using self-hypnosis."* Hollywood, Ca., Wilshire
    Co. 1961.

Glossary

ACCOUNTABILITY
> Therapists are held responsible for quality of care and length of treatment. Under managed care, they are monitored for performance of this responsibility.

ADAPTIVE FUNCTIONING
> This refers to the capability of acting and relating effectively in the workplace, at home, and at school. It generally means operating at or above a level of 71 on the Global Assessment of Functioning Scale (GAF Scale) in the *Diagnostic and Statistical Manual of Mental Disorders*. This is frequently the goal of treatment under managed care, and it is included in the definition of medical necessity under some benefit plans.

BACKWARD INTEGRATION
> When a company seeks to expand its functions in the marketplace, it often seeks to purchase or merge with others who precede its designated set of services. In the behavioral health care industry this usually means merging with others along the chain of referrals or chain of payment flow. For example, a hospital that previously focused exclusively upon the provision of treatment might sign a capitated contract, which would expand its services to include utilization management, evaluation, and referrals.

BIBLIOTHERAPY
> Utilization of books or workbooks as components of treatment.

CAPITATION
> Payment on a per-person basis. For example: agreement to treat any of 1000 employees for any behavioral health need for a month, with a reimbursement of $2.00 per employee. This would give the provider a total of $2000 for the care of any and all of the 1000 employees who utilize services during that month.

CAPITATION RATE

Amount of monthly reimbursement per employee in a capitated contract. In the above example, the capitated rate would be $2.00.

CARE MANAGEMENT

A program of screening for eligibility and appropriate utilization of treatment within the context of the patient's benefit structure. This may include helping to develop and/or implement a treatment strategy for the patient and/or the patient's family that is at times more inclusive than the individual provider's treatment with a particular patient.

CARVE OUT

The removal of one piece of a benefit program. For example: an employer may contract with an H.M.O. for all medical care and then "carve out" the behavioral health part, to contract separately with a P.P.O. for that care because of greater expertise or better access offered by the preferred provider organization.

CASE RATE

One payment rate regardless of the number of episodes of treatment. For example, a provider may have a case rate of $100 for a one-to-three-visit evaluation and brief treatment package. That provider will receive $100 if he sees the client one time. He will also receive $100 if he sees the client three times.

CLOSED PANEL

A network of preferred or exclusive providers that is full and therefore not accepting any new providers.

COB (COORDINATION OF BENEFITS)

When a patient is covered by two insurance companies for the same treatment, benefit payments must be adjusted so that the total payment does not exceed 100% of the total allowed under the mutual benefit structures.

COBRA (CONSOLIDATED OMNIBUS BUDGET RECONCILIATION ACT OF 1985)

A national legal regulation, which, among other provisions, allows an employee who is ending employment to continue with the same insurance program at the same rates for a limited amount of time. The employee must pay the full costs—including the amount previously paid by his employer.

CONCURRENT REVIEW

Case management examination of medical necessity, appropriate treatment, and other factors during the course of treatment, rather than before treatment begins or after treatment ends. This makes it possible to change the course of treatment if that is indicated.

CONTINUUM OF CARE

This refers to the need to ensure that uninterrupted care is available and provided at the appropriate level of intensity as treatment progresses. For example: a patient is hospitalized as a result of a need for detoxification. Once medically and psychologically stabilized, the patient may be "stepped down" to an intermediate-care facility and eventually to intensive or once-a-week outpatient treatment, as the appropriateness of each level of intervention is presented. Please see "Least Restrictive Level of Care."

COST CONTAINMENT

The effort to ensure that treatment is provided in the least expensive manner.

COST EFFECTIVE

An effort to produce the best possible outcome at the least possible cost.

COVERED LIVES

The number of people covered by a benefit plan.

DRGs (DIAGNOSIS RELATED GROUPS)

Groups of diagnoses lumped together by Medicare to determine rates of pay for hospital stays. All reimbursement is made on a cost-per-case basis, with cost established by the diagnosis at the time of admission. See "Prospective Pricing."

EPO (EXCLUSIVE PROVIDER ORGANIZATION)

An organization that contracts for care, in which enrollees must go only to the providers who are contracted with the plan, and no payment is made for treatment by any other provider. By way of contrast, those who enroll in preferred provider plans usually have a lower copayment and sometimes other benefits for going to a network-contracted provider, but they can — at greater expense — go to a non-network-contracted provider.

FACILITY-DRIVEN MANAGED CARE PRODUCTS

Some hospitals and other facilities are beginning to develop their own managed care subsidiaries. These usually contract directly with local employers for full managed care services, offering such inducements as discounted hospital care rates.

FEE-FOR-SERVICE

Payment is made on the basis of each incident of service (each psychotherapy session, for example).

FOCUS

Managed care emphasizes brief therapy, in which treatment is centered around a very narrowly defined issue.

GATEKEEPER

The person (such as a managed care intake clinician) or entity (such as a managed care company) who determines the appropriate treatment modality and referral source.

HOLD-HARMLESS CLAUSES

Clauses in some preferred provider contracts that designate who is held responsible for any contractual liability. Often these are written in such a way as to give the sole responsibility to the provider.

H.P.O. (HOSPITAL-PHYSICIAN ORGANIZATION)

An I.P.A. (Independent Practice Association) composed of physicians associated with a hospital. Often this is initiated by the hospital, and the hospital provides many of the management services for the I.P.A.

I.P.A. (INDEPENDENT PRACTICE ASSOCIATION)

An association of providers—usually from all disciplines—who contract as a group with managed care organizations. (One variation consists of the H.P.O.s noted above.) Often these organizations subcontract with M.C.O.s on a risk-share basis, making these organizations very attractive partners for some P.P.O.s

LEAST RESTRICTIVE LEVEL OF CARE

Care levels vary in cost and intensity, all the way from once-a-week outpatient to inpatient care. The standard of most-appropriate care for the managed care industry is "What is the least restrictive level of care?" This means finding the level of care that offers sufficient safety and effective treatment but the least restriction on the patient's activities and the least cost. Please see "Continuum of Care."

MANAGED BEHAVIORAL CARE

Mental health or chemical dependency treatment that is screened and monitored for meeting utilization criteria, treatment effectiveness, and/or quality.

NATURALLY OCCURRING THERAPY

Self-treatment occurring as a result of daily living. Examples include petting your cat, jogging, or normal self-affirmations.

OPEN PANEL

A list of approved providers for a managed care company that is not yet full. This may be a preferred provider panel, an exclusive provider panel, or any variation.

PASS THROUGH

A responsibility or service normally fulfilled by one level of managed care (see "Backward Integration") but given to a lower service level. For example: an explanation of what it means to employees to shift from an indemnity contract to a managed care contract is usually the responsibility of the benefits department. Often the managed care company or the provider of services is the entity that actually discharges this responsibility.

P.P.S (PROSPECTIVE PAYMENT SYSTEM)

See "Prospective Pricing."

PREAUTHORIZATION

Payment for most services provided to a beneficiary of a managed care contract will be made only after someone in the managed care company agrees that the treatment is needed and sanctions it.

PROSPECTIVE PRICING

Setting a specific total, all-inclusive price for a service prior to delivery of the service. This often applies on a diagnostic-related basis. For example: all inpatient treatment for substance abuse is priced at a set daily (per diem) rate, regardless of service-cost variance. These prices are usually set by the managed care plan or the payer and not by the provider.

PROVIDER

Any professional who furnishes ("provides") treatment to a covered patient. Preferred providers or exclusive providers are authorized to furnish treatment to covered enrollees. Facilities that offer professional services to covered patients are also sometimes referred to as providers.

QUALITY ASSURANCE

Efforts to measure performance toward a goal of optimal outcome are being undertaken by many businesses today. These measures are only in their formative development stages in behavioral health care at this time.

REGIONAL INTEGRATED SYSTEMS OF CARE

As the American Health Security Act comes closer to implementation, behavioral health personnel are feeling an increasing need to link together into regional networks, since contracts will probably be awarded on a regional basis. This means that provider groups, inpatient centers, intermediate-care facilities, local E.A.P.s, and many other organizations are beginning to link together to form seamless continuums of care.

RETROSPECTIVE REVIEW

Evaluation of services after treatment has concluded. This is usually a review of records, done on a random basis, to ensure consistency, appropriate documentation, and compliance with utilization parameters. It is sometimes used to understand patterns of treatment, but rarely results in retrospective denial of payment.

RISK POOL

The total number of people insured by any plan or group of plans. The larger the number of people insured, the greater chance of stable costs. If one person in a ten-employee group has a catastrophic illness, he can affect the costs of the group plan enormously. But if one person in a 10,000-employee group has a catastrophic illness, the costs may well be offset by a large number of employees who have no need to utilize the plan for treatment at all.

SELF-HELP ORGANIZATIONS

Nonprofessional groups set up by their participants to help themselves. For example: Alcoholics Anonymous, Parents and Friends of Lesbians and Gays, Parents without Partners, Exceptional Children's Foundation.

SELF-INSURED

A large company that pays for insurance claims out of its own funds instead of paying insurance premiums.

SUBSCRIBER

One who purchases behavioral health insurance; usually an employee. This is in contrast to other covered beneficiaries; usually dependents.

SYMPTOMATIC RELIEF

Much of managed care therapy is for the purpose of ameliorating targeted manifestations of pathological conditions or of distress. This is in contrast to the goal for therapists/patients when indemnity insurance was the primary payer: a cure or near-cure of the underlying psychodynamics that have led to the symptoms.

THIRD-PARTY PAYERS

Traditionally, we have thought of the therapeutic contract as applying to two parties: the patient/client and the therapist. However, when insurance is utilized there is a third party: the party whose function is payment. Managed care companies have positioned themselves as representatives of the third party—the payers.

TIME-LIMITED

Since little agreement occurs about what brief treatment is, more theorists are beginning to look at treatment in terms of its time limits and referring to it simply as "time-limited treatment."

TPA (THIRD-PARTY ADMINISTRATOR)

See "Third-Party Payers" above. Managed care companies that administer the provision of benefits for insurance companies position themselves to become third-party administrators.

TREATMENT PLANS

A delineation of and a format for reaching treatment goal(s).

TRIAGE

The process of assessing patients and referring them to the appropriate resource. This can include the process of prioritizing treatment.

UTILIZATION REVIEW

Review of services to determine whether or not they are medically necessary and appropriate.

Index

Balint, M., 59
Bargaining, and managed care, 4
Barron's, 21
Bartlett, Dr. John, 109
Behavioral health care
  competitive analysis of, 135–37
  cost escalation in, 6–7
  equality of coverage for, 117
  multispecialty groups for, 117
  psychotherapy and managed, 63–64
  vertical financing system of, 132
Behavioral Healthcare Tomorrow conference, 28
Behavioral Healthcare Tomorrow Journal, 22
Behavioral health hospitals, marketing departments of, 23
Behavioral health professional, ascertaining quality of, 87–88
Behavioral therapy, 58
"Benchmarking," 107
Benchmarks, 108
Benefit flexibility, bias against, 93
Benefits, notification of changes in, 95–96, 99
Benefit sophistication, 66–68
  quality checklist for, 75
Benefits Today, 21
Benefit structure, actuarial-based, 67
Bereavement therapy, 127
Bibilotherapy, utilization of, 72–73
Biodyne, 81
Board Certified Diplomates, 17
Books, written/read, 49
Boroughs, Lizabet, M., 19
Brief therapy, 58–59
  training for, 152
Brown bag lunch presentation, 42
Business goals, statement of, 140–43

  See also Goal(s); Goal Setting
Business Insurance, 22
Business terminology, as used by managed care, 30

Cagney, Tamara, 106, 108
California, regulations re. provider network, 14
California Association of Marriage and Family Therapists, 104
"California Therapist, The," 104
Capitation, 91
  defined, 105
  factors in assessing, 105–6
  as payment mechanism, 116
Cardiff, Maureen, 82–83
Care
  continuity of, 36
  See also Continuation of care
  guidelines for level of, 71
Career planning, 53
Case fee reimbursement, 106
Case manager
  and additional referrals, 47
  contact with, 37–38
  sophistication of, 97, 100
  and therapists' attitudes, 65–66
  and treatment decision appeals, 94, 99
Case rates, 91
Certifications, 49
Chamber of Commerce, 150–51
Changes, near-term, 103–10
Chemical dependency, training for treatment of, 152
CIGNA, 102
Claims processing procedures, 96, 99
Clinical input, as paramount, 92
Clinical linking consistency, quality check-list for, 76